Mission Transition

Mission Transition

Managing Your Career and Your Retirement

JANET I. FARLEY

ROWMAN & LITTLEFIELD
Lanham • Boulder • New York • London

Published by Rowman & Littlefield
A wholly owned subsidiary of The Rowman & Littlefield Publishing Group, Inc.
4501 Forbes Boulevard, Suite 200, Lanham, Maryland 20706
www.rowman.com

Unit A, Whitacre Mews, 26-34 Stannary Street, London SE11 4AB

British Library Cataloguing in Publication Information Available

Library of Congress Cataloging-in-Publication Data
Names: Farley, Janet I., author.
Title: Mission transition : managing your career and your retirement / Janet
   I. Farley.
Other titles: Managing your career and your retirement
Description: Lanham, MD : Rowman & Littlefield, [2018] | Includes
   bibliographical references and index.
Identifiers: LCCN 2017016563 (print) | LCCN 2017019456 (ebook) | ISBN
   9781442281622 (electronic) | ISBN 9781442281615 (cloth : alk. paper)
Subjects: LCSH: Retired military personnel—Employment—United States. |
   Veterans—Employment—United States. | Military pensions—United States. |
   Career changes—United States.
Classification: LCC UB357 (ebook) | LCC UB357 .F37 2018 (print) | DDC
   646.7/908835500973—dc23
LC record available at https://lccn.loc.gov/2017016563

♾™ The paper used in this publication meets the minimum requirements of
American National Standard for Information Sciences—Permanence of Paper
for Printed Library Materials, ANSI/NISO Z39.48-1992.

Printed in the United States of America

This book is dedicated to those who have served in the United States Armed Forces and to those who have supported them on the home front.

Contents

Acknowledgments

As a general rule, it is appreciated by other authors that the process of writing a book is not an easy one. Even if you have divine inspiration and a driving ambition to spread the word on good stuff that genuinely matters, it is still really hard work that is both time and life consuming. It certainly doesn't happen without the gracious support of others, and the process of writing this particular book was no exception.

First and foremost, I owe a great deal of thanks to Kathryn Knigge, associate editor at Rowman & Littlefield, for her continued support and patience. I am grateful for her genuine concern for our military service members and their families and for her admirable willingness to create good books for them. Thanks are likewise given to Patricia Stevenson, production editor, for moving the manuscript forward in the publication process.

I am also grateful to the team of many unnamed, yet highly appreciated, professionals at Rowman & Littlefield who spent their valuable time reading, editing, designing, and launching this book into the world. These unsung publishing heroes are awesome, and all the behind-the-scenes hard work, expertise, and dedication are very much appreciated.

While I consider myself fairly guru-like on military-to-civilian career transition topics, I do not in any way, shape, or form claim to be a financial expert at this point in my career. This book does, however, focus on financial matters as they relate to the military transition process. Lucky for us, I happen to know a few great financial experts, and they were graciously willing to share their expertise with me in this book.

In writing chapter 2, "A Crash Course Plus in the Blended Retirement System," I reached out to a few of my favorite financial experts for their sage advice and wisdom, and they reached back. I am so grateful to them for their willingness to contribute their expertise and advice to the readers of this book.

Specifically, heartfelt thanks go to Mr. Joseph "J.J." Montanaro, CFP, the relationship director of the Military Advocacy Group for USAA; Mr. Shane Ostrom, CFP, deputy director of finance and benefits information for the Military Officers Association of America (MOAA); Mrs. Starlett Henderson, AFC, who is a veteran and family member employment specialist; Mr. Doug Nordman, author of *The Military Guide to Financial Independence and Retirement* and *The Military Financial Independence and Retirement Pocket Guide*; and Mrs. Attiyya Ingram, AFC, who is the owner of Ingram Financial Management. I greatly respect and appreciate all of your professional expertise, your own personal military service and family member experiences, and your selfless dedication to helping others.

I must also say thank you to Mrs. Kelly Buchfink, a financial advisor for First Command Financial Services, and Mrs. Jackie Nasca, an independent financial counselor, for their insights when asked and for further leads that helped me to craft this book in areas where I consider them the experts. I'm also very glad that they are my longtime friends.

I'd like to thank Mr. Wayne Boswell, who recently retired as the DoD's financial readiness director, for pointing me in the right direction to learn more about the military's new Blended Retirement System at a time when finding information on it wasn't quite as easy as it is now. I'd also like to acknowledge him here for his lifelong service and faithful commitment to all our service members and their families. I had the great honor of working for Mr. Boswell at Headquarters, European Command, in Stuttgart, Germany, with the J1 Quality of Life Program, and I know that his skilled ability to connect diverse groups of people, craft meaningful policy, and make a positive difference will be sorely missed by many in federal service.

To all those other federal employees, military service members, military family members, contracted service providers, military family advocacy organizations, and private industry employers out there who do more than they have to for our service members and their families, both because it's the right thing to do and because they know that doing their part well, regardless of its size, will contribute to the greater good somewhere along the line, I say thank you, too.

While I didn't directly contact anyone at Blue Star Families for assistance with this book, I did find their 2016 Military Family Lifestyle Survey extremely helpful. You'll find it referenced throughout the book. I, as both a military spouse and an author, am grateful for the timely research and advocacy that they do on behalf of service members and military families.

Much love and appreciation goes to my family, my favorite people ever. To say that this past year in our lives has been eventful would be a gross understatement. After living what seems like a lifetime abroad between military and federal service, we transitioned ourselves from one side of the world to the other. Much like the process of writing a book, we found that it just wasn't easy. Change, it would seem, never is. Still, throughout the many challenges of global repatriation, my favorite peeps rose to the occasion and cheered me on to the finish line as they have done before.

I'm not sure how many grande mochas my daughter Frannie brought me from Starbucks, but there were more than a few, and they helped to motivate me accordingly. My other daughter, Terrie, always knew when to leave me an encouraging note or give me a "you got this" fist pump. Farley, my husband, was very encouraging and had an uncanny ability to know when to suggest ordering takeout for dinner. Even my dog got in on the support act by keeping my feet warm as I pounded out chapters on my laptop. #MyFamily #GottaLoveThem #IDoIReallyDo

Finally, I am extremely grateful to you, the reader, for holding this book in your hands. It was an honor to write it. I sincerely hope that it makes a positive difference in some way, shape, or form for you or for someone you care about.

Introduction

Your current job in uniform is fairly demanding, am I right?

When you're not busy packing your bags for yet another deployment to some faraway place and painfully saying good-bye to those you love again or enduring long hours at work wherever you happen to be stationed, you occasionally catch yourself daydreaming about your future.

Admit it. *We all do it.*

One day, you think, you'll transition out of service, maybe even retire if you get the energy and have the good fortune to serve a full twenty years. After you get out, you will easily land a great civilian job with an amazing employer who appreciates your ever-winning warrior-like ways.

You may not have a clear grip on all the details just now, but you do know that you won't have to worry about moving every few years anymore, so you will settle down. You and your better half will buy a nice little house somewhere on a nice little street in some nice little town. It will be . . . *nice.*

You will finally be in charge of your own destiny.

Your spouse will be eternally grateful and able to finally land a real job that offers career advancement and professional satisfaction.

Your children will never have to be the new kids in school anymore. They will finish growing up with a sense of stability, the likes of which they have never experienced before.

Even your dog will like to be around you again.

Who's the alpha? You are, big guy. You are. *Woof.*

And how exactly will your encore career look in this altered dimension?

You will, of course, work normal hours, wear normal clothes, and get paid extremely well for it. You will be a corporate force with which to be reckoned.

You will be a card-carrying member of Easy Street, and it will be epic.

Of course, your own happy post-uniform daydream may not look exactly like this one, but you probably do have one floating around somewhere in your subconscious. Getting it from daydream to reality can be a challenge, however.

WHY IT'S SO HARD TO TRANSITION

Serving in the United States military, or being the significant other of someone who does, has never been a job for the faint of heart. It is a tough life with its fair share of adventure and more than its fair share of hardship and challenge.

When the military family is your family, regardless of your role in it, you become a part of a much bigger story. The headlines heard on the evening news about events that happen in faraway places are often more than just interesting information. They are the very stuff your life is all about. A family member I once interviewed said it perfectly when he commented that while other people were busy reading about history, he was busy living it.

Maybe that is one of the many reasons why transitioning out of the military, whether you are a service member or a family member, is so hard.

When you retire or transition out of service, you are not just leaving a job behind. You are leaving a mission- and service-oriented way of life behind, too. As a result, that time period from when you first decide to leave military life until well after you are already out of it can be an emotional, logistical, and financial challenge unlike any you may have experienced before.

Don't worry, though. You're up for it.

You know, for example, that getting out of service will probably be harder than it was to get in it in the first place. There will no doubt be countless numbers of forms to sign, briefings to attend, and important benefits to learn about.

Then, of course, there is the whole issue of timing. When should you start the process of getting out? When will you be able to go to the Transition Assistance Program (TAP) office and use their services?

And what exactly are you going to do when you do get out? Do you want or need to start a new job right away, or do you plan to go to college? Are you taking some much-needed time off? Can you even afford to get out of the military?

What exactly do the cards have in mind for you?

If you are planning on getting a job, how long will it take you to line up job interviews? How do you even do that in the first place? What type of resume do you need and how should you dress? Will you fit in at the new workplace, and what if you don't?

What if civilian life isn't all you thought it would be?

AS IF THERE ISN'T ENOUGH TO THINK ABOUT ALREADY . . .

Add to those complicated issues the much-anticipated arrival on January 1, 2018, of the military's new Blended Retirement System (BRS), replacing the traditional legacy retirement pension, and the odds of being overwhelmed by all the moving parts become even greater.

What does the BRS mean for you and your family? Does it even apply? Do you have to opt in? What happens when you leave the military? When are you able to access your savings? How do you know how much to even save? What happens to the funds in your Thrift Savings Plan (TSP) account, if anything?

There are many, many retirement, career transition, and work/life adjustment questions to consider. Many of them potentially have multiple answers, depending on who you are and where you happen to be in your life at any given moment.

Lucky for you, there is no need to go into vapor lock. You're moving in the right direction already by holding this book in your hands.

Mission Transition: Managing Your Career and Your Retirement is a concise and user-friendly guide designed to help you to cope with the new and not-so-new issues you have to deal with as you transition out.

WHO CAN BENEFIT THE MOST FROM THIS BOOK?

If you are currently serving in uniform, this book is written for you, first and foremost. It's written as if you and I were sitting across the table from each other, discussing each topic in person.

I have to warn you: I tend to tell it like I see it, whether you happen to like it or not. If you were to ask any of the many service members I have worked with before if this is a bad thing, I believe they would tell you that it is not. It is a good thing, and it means I care about you. I want you to succeed, and I want you to know all the facts first, for better or worse.

You aren't the only one who can benefit from *Mission Transition*, however. Your spouse or significant other will as well. Whether she or he serves in uniform or not, service and sacrifice is a given.

Military service, as you know better than anyone, isn't a job for those seeking quick riches or an easy day's work. What you do doesn't truly compare to what others do, does it, now? Nor does being married to someone in the military or raising a family around it. Sacrifices, of the paid or unpaid variety, are made daily.

Multiple deployments and family separations are a hard fact of life. Frequent relocations upend any illusions of personal and professional stability. These are just a few of the stressors you and your family have probably experienced.

The bottom line in a military marriage, on paper or in matters of the heart, is that you are a team, and the best teams succeed when everyone knows the situation at hand for what it is and shares in the responsibility of crafting the game plan for moving forward.

You will also find this book helpful if you are someone who is thinking about joining the military or marrying into it. As you may discover soon enough, change in the military lifestyle is a given, and keeping up with it can be a real challenge. Not keeping up with it, however, can be a big mistake, having a long-lasting and negative impact on you and your family. You should know, before you sign on, what you may be getting yourself into on a financial and post-uniform transitional level. Great care has been taken to explain some military-related concepts and assumptions throughout the book with you in mind.

If you happen to be one of the many dedicated service providers working across the globe in support of our military service members and their families in family centers, in and out processing centers, and Transition Assistance Programs, then this book is written for you, too. *Mission Transition* would make a great addition to your reference shelf and a fabulous purchase in bulk for your service member clients. You, after all, are the invisible front line that assures our uniformed service members and their families that you know the policies, programs, and benefits available to them. Without clear guidance and genuine understanding on your part, new programs, policies, and laws get horribly lost in translation, and that's not good for anybody.

WHAT IS IN STORE FOR YOU HERE

Let's be clear: The introduction of the Blended Retirement System, and the (pardon the pun) retirement of the legacy retirement system, is a big deal. You want to keep up with all the changes. The health and well-being of your financial future depends on it. All the changes may seem confusing and overwhelming at first. Anything new on such a grand scale usually is. There will be, however, lots of explanations forthcoming to you from many different directions.

You're going to be inundated with ample Department of Defense (DoD)–created information on the topic, and that's a good thing. Read everything you can get your hands on (including this book, of course).

What will make this book a little different from the deluge of fact sheets that will wind up in your inbox, on your doorstep, and in countless training modules you are sure to be required to complete is that this book looks at more than just the new retirement system.

This book doesn't simply outline the basic facts for you. It encourages you to look at the big picture that is your career and your future afterlife as a civilian. Consider it a caring whisper in your ear that says:

- Things are truly changing concerning your pay and you need to know about them and understand how they will affect you personally.
- You might think you will stay in uniform forever, but you won't. You may serve twenty-plus years and retire, experiencing a very different retirement pay setup than your pre-2018 predecessors. Or you may only serve a couple of years, but guess what? Your transition out of the military, either way, is something you need to proactively think about and plan for on many levels.

Mission Transition is here to help you do just that.

The book is divided into three parts, covering the military's new Blended Retirement System, the mechanics of a military-to-civilian career transition, and the adjustment to life as a civilian.

In part I, "The Changing Definition of Retirement in the Military," chapter 1, "Retirement: One Word. Two Definitions," we will discuss the evolving definition of *retirement* in the military. We will compare and contrast the concept of the word between the military and the civilian worlds and stress the importance of embracing an expanding definition of it as it relates to life outside of the uniform. We will also begin our conversation about the military's new Blended Retirement System and drive home the importance of being more than superficially financially literate as a result.

In chapter 2, "A Crash Course Plus in the Blended Retirement System," we will get into the nuts and bolts of the plan, giving you a crash course in simple English on the topic. You will learn the finer details you need to know about the new and improved Thrift Savings Plan (TSP), the ins and outs of continuation pay, and the continued role of annuities, along with the option for a lump sum at retirement for those who make it to twenty or more years of service.

We'll also hear from several trusted financial experts who have ample experience working within the military community. If you have a choice regarding whether to opt in to the new BRS, you will appreciate reading their thoughts, based on their years of financial expertise. It may help you as you go through your own decision-making process.

Finally, in this chapter, you will also be provided a timely list (at least as of publication date) of trustworthy online resources and calculators to help you plot and plan what is best for you.

In part II, "Moving from Where You Are to Where You Want to Be," and more specifically in chapter 3, "The Space in Between Worlds," we will turn our attention to the actual transition process itself. It is a big one that demands full commitment from you, in your heart and in your mind. We will discuss how you can get to that comfortable spot inside of you.

Before you get out of uniform, you have to check off a number of blocks in the eyes of the DoD. In this chapter, we will look closely at the motions you have to go through in order to become a civilian again. You will also get a significant overview of your potential post-uniform benefits and entitlements as well as a laundry list of transition resources that you can use in the process. The important topic of being financially fit enough to transition out of service will likewise be touched on.

In chapter 4, "Job Hunting 101: Practical Tips to Help You Get Hired," you'll discover (or perhaps review) how to find a good job as you transition out of uniform. Specifically, we'll cover the importance of having a clue from the beginning. You'll learn how to identify and apply for jobs. You'll figure out what makes a good resume an even better one. You'll learn how to effectively interview for a job, using the language of those who don't wear a uniform. You'll also learn what can be negotiated and how it can be negotiated. Finally, you'll learn how to graciously accept or decline all those job offers sure to come your way.

In part III, "Making Your New Normal Work," comprising chapter 5, "Strategies for Success on the New Job," you'll learn how to make a good first impression during the first one hundred days of your new job. We'll also discuss the importance of planning ahead to your next career move. In this chapter, we'll talk about civilian life outside of the workplace. It can take a while to feel comfortable in your new civilian skin, and sometimes the need for professional assistance arises. This chapter will offer you ideas and strategies for those occasions.

In the appendices of this book, you will find financial-, transition-, and career-related resource links and a glossary of commonly used terms in the book.

THIS BOOK IS DIFFERENT AND WHY

This book is different because it encourages you to think beyond the concept of simply transitioning out of service. It encourages you to think about the quality of life you want for the long term and how you are going to get it. It stresses not only the importance of effectively marketing the professional skills you learned in the military but also the importance of really understanding and managing your finances.

Too often, service members and spouses who are retiring or transitioning out of service isolate the issues and, in doing so, shortchange themselves in the long run. For example, it is easy to get caught up in worrying about finding a new job and forget to pay attention to time-sensitive benefits that may require your attention sooner rather than later. A synthesis of big-picture thought and intentional planning and action will prevent that from happening.

Mission Transition works hard to get you to look at the big picture. It is a book unlike any other currently available at the moment. It is my sincerest hope that this book helps you to understand the facts about the Blended Retirement System and that it helps you to put the big-picture topics of retirement (whether yours will be a military one or not), career transition, and adjustment to civilian life in better perspective.

WHAT THIS BOOK WON'T DO FOR YOU

Mission Transition is a great book that will give you the important information you need to move forward in your own transition. As great as it is, however, it will not do everything for you.

It will not make your decisions for you. *You have to do that.*

It will not give you all the answers to your questions, either. You may have to dig deeper to find the right answers for you and your specific situation.

It will not be a step-by-step financial guide for you to follow. It will offer you the facts, stats, theories, and helpful suggestions. If you want hard-core financial advice, please seek a hard-core financial expert.

It will not guarantee you life on Easy Street when you ultimately hit the universally accepted definition of retirement, assuming that event is one you subscribe to in the first place. While it will not guarantee you a financially comfortable life, it may give you the red flag warning you need now to best prepare for such a life later.

ABOUT MY CREDENTIALS, ASSUMPTIONS, AND BEST INTENTIONS

Mission Transition is written by someone who comes from the same world you live in now or the one you are thinking of joining.

As a U.S. Marine Corps brat, an army wife, and a career consultant with more than twenty-three years of military-to-civilian and military spouse employment expertise, I care deeply about your and your family's transition success because I know how special you are. I know how hard you work and how much you and your family have sacrificed. I know that service and sacrifice are not simply stand-alone events that happen in time. Rather, they are daily occurrences in your life that those unaccustomed to them may never understand. In the end, that's okay. Maybe they aren't really meant to understand this particular way of life anyway.

Throughout the book, you may see service members or job seekers referred to in either the masculine or the feminine form. No offense to anyone of any gender intended here. One or the other form is used to keep writing uncomplicated and flowing.

This book is not intended to give you specific legal, financial, or tax-related advice. There are professional lawyers, skilled financial planners, and certified public accountants for that, and I encourage you to hire them or take advantage of any such available services on the military installation nearest you.

The Blended Retirement System is a new system, and there is an ever-growing body of material out there about it. In the early stages of researching the topic and drafting this book, it was particularly problematic to nail down clear facts simply because they were not available at the time. Even when they were published, they were sometimes revised in short order. Please know that every effort has been made within the pages of this book to provide you with the most accurate facts available about the Blended Retirement System, the military-to-civilian career transition process, and everything else, for that matter. If any errors should be discovered, please accept my humble apologies.

It *is* the intention of this book, *Mission Transition*, to get you thinking about your transition in holistic terms, incorporating the universal (and not just the military) idea of retirement into your planning thought processes for your future. It is also the intention of this book to show you the first steps you need to take to move toward your life outside of the military and to thrive in your new job and in your new civilian life.

I would love to hear from you if you feel those intentions hit their marks or even if you think that they didn't. Please feel free to contact me with your thoughts, comments, and/or suggestions for future editions through the publisher, Rowman & Littlefield.

I

THE CHANGING DEFINITION OF RETIREMENT IN THE MILITARY

Retirement

One Word. Two Definitions.

To those who selflessly serve our country in uniform and to those eternally patient souls married to or partnered with them, the word *retirement* means something different than it does to their civilian counterparts living outside the shroud of a camouflaged world.

For the vast majority of those who serve twenty or more years and actually retire from the military,[1] it is commonly noted as a singular event in time signifying blessed freedom from being told what to do, when to do it, and how to do it.

When a service member makes it through the years in uniform to military retirement, it is reason for celebration. The brass ring has been captured and lifelong benefits solidified. Traditional military retirement benefits, after all, are the top reason that 63 percent of service members continue to stay in the military.[2]

It means the kitschy plastic retirement countdown clock (with a picture of the invitingly blue ocean, beach chair, and cool fruity beverage on it) that has been sitting on your desk for the last year has no days left to count down to anymore. You have made it, doing more than your fair share in a demanding career field. Congratulations. You are in charge of buying the rounds for everyone in the bar that particular night.

It has also come to mean a monthly pension paycheck to the small minority of service members who have actually reached the Big R. To the 81 percent of

service members who do not make it to military retirement,[3] either by choice
or by fate, there is no monthly paycheck after time in service—just the rollover
of the Thrift Savings Plan (TSP) and whatever other savings they have managed
to accumulate.

Typically, when someone retires from the military, he looks for a next
job because he still has bills to pay and possibly mouths to feed. He usually
doesn't while away the days until his final demise and start collecting social
security anytime soon—unless, of course, he happens to be very senior in
rank and long in years at the time of his retirement.

For example's sake, let us assume you entered military service at the tender
young age of eighteen years and you survived/served in uniform for twenty
honorable years. In such a case, you would potentially be eligible for a military retirement from the Department of Defense (DoD) at the ripe old age
of thirty-eight, or what many in mainstream society would view as the very
prime of your working life.

The concept of retirement outside the military, by contrast, is another
animal altogether, and an ever-changing one at that, as baby boomers deftly
defy society's traditionally expected norms and boldly continue slaving away
among generations in the workforce until their last breath.

According to the Social Security Administration (SSA), "Full retirement
age is the age at which a person may become entitled to full or unreduced
retirement benefits."[4] The SSA states that individuals may start receiving
benefits as early as sixty-two years of age or as late as seventy years of age.[5]

When healthy civilians do finally "retire," they travel the world for fun (or
maybe to do good works). They may go fishing. They might play bridge on
Monday nights and golf in the mornings before the sun gets too hot. They
at least think they will do all those things they said they would do when they
had time.

Or they may do nothing because they simply can't afford to do anything.
They're too busy paying off their children's college loans or trying to recover
from unwise financial choices made in the distant or not-so-distant past. (It's
even more depressing for unhealthy retirees who face old age with the specter
of rising health care costs and dwindling resources.)

Generally speaking, civilians who have decided to retire and kick back to
whatever quality of life awaits them aren't busy creating marketable resumes

and seeking out new employers, unless they absolutely have to do so for financial or mental reasons.

So we can see clearly that one little word, *retirement*, has two different meanings depending upon your perspective. Unless you've been living in a very isolated foxhole, you know the traditional definition of retirement within the military is changing at warp speed. And if you want to live happily ever after in your golden years, then you're going to have to change your thought processes along the way.

Not only does the concept of retirement differ between the military and the civilian worlds, but now it doesn't mean exactly what it used to in the military, either.

THE WAIT IS OVER AND THE BRS IS HERE

If you are serving in uniform, then you already know a thing or two about the military's new Blended Retirement System (BRS). It has certainly been in the news recently and will most likely stay in the Department of Defense (DoD) headlines for at least a couple more years as the system is officially rolled out and institutionalized for the applicable masses.

Chapter 2, "A Crash Course Plus in the Blended Retirement System," will launch into the finer details of the system, but, for now, here are the policy highlights you need to know.

The BRS was created by the Fiscal Year 2016 National Defense Authorization Act in an effort to blend the military's traditional legacy retirement pension with a defined contribution to the service members' Thrift Savings Plan account.

It goes into effect on January 1, 2018.

If you are a military service member who is serving as of December 31, 2017, then you are covered under the legacy retirement system. No one, according to the DoD, who is currently serving will be automatically switched to the BRS.

Some of you, however, have a choice in the matter.

Even though you may be covered under the old retirement system, active-duty component service members with less than twelve years of service since their pay entry date and reserve component service members who have accrued fewer than 4,320 retirement points as of December 31, 2017, will have

The U.S. Uniformed Services Blended Retirement System

At a Glance

Saving with the New Blended Retirement System

The Fiscal Year 2016 National Defense Authorization Act provides our military force with a modernized retirement plan built for retirement savings. Beginning in 2018, our service members can get **automatic and matching Thrift Savings Plan contributions** as well as mid-career **compensation incentives** in addition to monthly **annuities for life.** All service members under the current system are grandfathered into today's retirement system.

Today's Retirement System:

Annuity

2.5% x Years Served x Retired Pay Base
after completing 20 years of service

---

1 Automatic and Matching Contributions

Automatic contributions are seen immediately

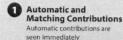

You Contribute	DoD Auto Contribution	DoD Matches	Total
0%	1%	0%	1%
1%	1%	1%	3%
2%	1%	2%	5%
3%	1%	3%	7%
4%	1%	3.5%	8.5%
5%	1%	4%	10%

The DoD automatically contributes **1%** of your basic pay to your **Thrift Savings Plan** after **60 days of service.**

You'll see matching contributions at the start of 3 through the completion of 26 years of service, and...

You're fully vested—it's yours to keep—as of the beginning of 3 years of service and goes with you when you leave.

2 Continuation Pay

Received at the mid-career point

You may receive a **cash payment** in exchange for additional service.

3 Full Retired Pay Annuity

Received after completing 20 years of service

 2% x **Years Served** x **Retired Pay Base**

Calculate your **retired pay base** by **averaging the highest 36 months of basic pay.** You'll gain this monthly annuity for life after completing 20 years of service.

Options for Collecting Your Retired Pay

Active Component	Reserve Component
Full retired pay annuity	Full retired pay annuity beginning at age 60*

or

Lump sum with reduced retired pay
50% or 25% of monthly retired pay annuity bumps back up to 100% at full retirement age (67 in most cases).

Could be earlier based on credited active service

Effective Date of the New System

January 1 2018

Your Retirement System
If you joined the service...

▸ **After December 31, 2017**
You'll be automatically enrolled in the Blended Retirement System.

▸ **After December 31, 2005 but before January 1, 2018**
You'll have the choice to enroll in the Blended Retirement System or remain in today's current retirement system.

▸ **Before January 1, 2006**
You'll be grandfathered and remain in today's current retirement system.

Additional information coming soon.
Sources: Sections 631, 632, 633, 634, and 635 of the Fiscal Year 2016 National Defense Authorization Act.

Created 12/2015

Source: Sections 631, 632, 633, 634, and 635 of the Fiscal Year 2016 National Defense Authorization Act

the ability to opt into the BRS or remain under the legacy retirement system. If this happens to be you, then you have a specified, limited one-year period of time to say that you want in. The opt-in/election period for you begins on January 1, 2018, and concludes on December 31, 2018. If you fall into this category, you have probably already been to an "opt-in" class through your unit or taken the class online.

All service members who enter the military on or after January 1, 2018, will be automatically enrolled in the BRS.[6] Those who enter the service on or after January 1, 2018, and who become careerists serving twenty years or more will receive 20 percent less in lifetime annuities than their brothers and sisters who fell under or chose to stay with the legacy retirement system. With the BRS, however, the government will match contributions to the Thrift Savings Plan of up to 5 percent of basic pay.

Additionally, when service members reach twelve years of service, they will be eligible for something called continuation pay, which is a direct cash payout (much like a bonus). According to DoD guidance, active component members will be eligible for a cash incentive of 2.5–13 times their regular monthly basic pay, and reserve component members will be eligible for 0.5–6 times their monthly basic pay (as if serving on active duty), in return for a commitment of four more years of service.[7]

Why a New Retirement System? Why Now?

Blame it on the ever-increasing pension, health care, manpower, and training costs to the DoD.

Let's digress for a moment and run some numbers, shall we?

The Department of Defense is essentially the nation's largest employer, employing more than 1.4 million active-duty service members and 1.1 million reservists. Paying the salaries and associated benefits (to include health care) of those millions can be costly, and that's not all the DoD is paying for, either. It also employs 861,000 civilian employees around the globe and takes care of veterans and their families.

In addition to skyrocketing personnel costs, it maintains 561,975 facilities at 4,800 sites on twenty-five million acres. It has 250,000 vehicles, 5,285 aircraft, and 293 ships.[8] Its budget for FY 2017 is $523.9 billion,[9] and chances are good it will exceed that budget, if history is to be believed.

According to a recent Congressional Budget Office presentation, the cost of developing and buying weapons (a useful expenditure for our armed forces) has been 20–30 percent higher than the DoD estimates. The costs of providing military pay and benefits to active and retired personnel have been increasing since 2000. If that isn't enough, the operation and maintenance costs per active-duty service member have been steadily increasing since at least 1980, without including the costs of the wars in Iraq and Afghanistan.[10]

Cha-ching, Cha-ching, Cha-ching

At some point, someone decided the bleeding had to be stopped. Great minds felt that there had to be a way to encourage retention and cut costs at the same time. The Military Retirement Modernization Commission (MRMC) was then formed to find efficiencies in military pay and compensation.[11]

The committee deliberated long and hard. Their final efforts were published in January 2015 in a final report to Congress. The long-term study highlighted in the report included a harsh and unprecedented spotlight on the military retirement benefit in all its glory. Ultimately, that commission made its recommendations to Congress, contending that the existing legacy retirement system was unfair to the masses, 81 percent of the total force,[12] who served honorably but not for twenty or more years.[13] Those recommendations were included in the National Defense Authorization Act of 2016, scheduled to become effective in 2018.

The "sacred cow" of military retirement pay had effectively become a steak on the grill, cooked well done, although some might eventually debate even that.

Is It a Good Thing for Service Members?

This is a fair question that deserves an honest answer. Unfortunately, it is much too soon to give you an honest and complete answer. Time will have to tell us.

If you do your research, however, you will definitely see that there are varying opinions on the topic out there now concerning whether it is a good deal for service members and whether it is a good deal for force retention in general.

The MRMC's final report showed that 80.2 percent of active-duty service members preferred the then-proposed new compensation plans, saying that "service members recognize the increased benefit of alternative compensation systems" and "they would prefer the modernized compensation system detailed [in this report] over the status quo by a margin of 4 to 1.5. While being more preferable, the proposed compensation system improves fiscal sustainability, providing a win-win solution for Service members and the Services."[14]

Another study commissioned by the U.S. Marine Corps concluded that the BRS "won't endanger force retention under any reasonable set of economic and behavioral assumptions."[15] This particular study further suggested "that young career-minded service members who opt into the new system, to get government-matching of their Thrift Savings Plan contributions, will still have potential career retirement benefits that most civilian peers would envy."[16]

On the flip side, a Financial Behaviors Index from First Command Financial Services Inc. reported that 73 percent of career service members who were *eligible* to be grandfathered into the legacy system *wanted* to be grandfathered into it.[17]

Right now, there are conflicting thoughts on either side of the "is the BRS good for you?" question. For more thoughts on whether this would be a good thing for you and your family, see chapter 2, "A Crash Course Plus in the Blended Retirement System."

Ultimately, it will be up to you to make it work, if you opt into it or if you have no choice. Making it work effectively, however, will call for a certain level of financial readiness and literacy, which could be a real problem for some service members and their families.

THE IMPORTANCE OF LIFELONG FINANCIAL LITERACY

Financial literacy has been a topic of concern within the DoD and within military family households for some time, and it should be, particularly now, when the onus of retirement planning within and far beyond the military years will fall squarely on the shoulders of troops and their families.

The big question of the day is simple: *Are military service members and families financially literate?*

If you were to shake the Magic 8 Ball and ask that question, chances are good it would tell you, "Situation not clear."

According to a Harris Poll survey created for the National Foundation for Credit Counseling, service members rate themselves highly on the topic but would welcome more advice and information.[18] Other interesting points to note from the same survey:

- Compared to the national population, service members are more cautious about what they spend and are more likely to save.
- They are also more likely to rely on and potentially misuse credit cards than U.S. adults. (According to the 2016 Blue Star Families Military Family Lifestyle Survey, 38 percent of active-duty service members have more credit card debt than the average American.)[19]
- Service members report having positive lending experiences but have had to occasionally look outside the traditional system for loans.
- Most who were surveyed expressed concerns about being financially prepared for the future, an emergency, or an unexpected event.

In the 2013 Quick Compass of Financial Issues survey conducted by the Defense Manpower Data Center (DMDC), 43 percent of service members indicated that they were able to make ends meet without much difficulty. Twenty-four percent said that they were very comfortable and secure, and 23 percent said they occasionally had some difficulty making ends meet. Nine percent said it was tough to make ends meet but they were keeping their heads above water, and 1 percent said that they were in over their heads.[20]

Some surveys conducted would seem to suggest that the higher the rank of the service member, the higher the financial literacy rate. That makes some degree of sense, as the higher the rank, the better the paycheck.

Younger service members and their spouses, if they have them, may have it more difficult, financially speaking, as paychecks are lower and life experiences with money more limited.

Is this a generalization? Sure it is. A larger paycheck and more maturity (theoretically, anyway) doesn't automatically translate into a higher level of financial literacy. There are plenty of mid- to senior-level service members who can blow through their paychecks with the best of them.

On a positive note, however, anyone (regardless of age, rank, and experience) can successfully up his money smarts with a little effort.

Statistics and surveys aside, one thing is clear: Financial education is crucial to your financial well-being, today and certainly in the long term.

There are definite benefits to being financially literate:

- You have a genuine understanding of how money works and are then more adept to make good financial decisions about your future. (Can you say *Blended Retirement System*?)
- When you are financially fit, you can focus better on your military mission and not spend valuable time worrying about your finances.
- Better family relations happen when money, including the lack or mismanagement of it, isn't the main topic of daily conversation.
- Some statistics suggest that increased levels of financial literacy (resulting in less internal stress) among service members could also lower suicide rates.
- You protect your government security clearance (if you have one) by being in good financial shape. If you can't live within your means, manage debt, or meet your financial obligations, then you come off as someone who doesn't know how to be in control. This is never good for your current job or for your future outlook professionally. It also makes you a potential target for blackmail by nefarious characters, which, again, is never good for your current job or for your future outlook professionally.

When you have a good understanding of your own financial situation, where you are now, where you want to be, and how you're going to get there, you can move forward more positively in your life, your military-to-civilian career transition, and ultimately your own retirement in your golden years.

To its credit, the DoD seems to understand that "those with higher [financial] literacy are more likely to plan for retirement and to have an emergency fund, and less likely to engage in expensive credit card behaviors."[21]

The new fact of life, whether you are retiring from the military or transitioning out, is that the bigger picture of your personal retirement one day is fully your responsibility. The decisions you make regarding your own financial situation could impact you and your family, for better or worse, later.

Self Check:
How Financially Fit Is Your Household?

Read each statement and place an X by either TRUE or FALSE.

	TRUE	FALSE
1. We have a spending plan (a budget) in place.	_____	_____
2. We pay our bills on time, all the time.	_____	_____
3. We do not struggle to live from paycheck to paycheck.	_____	_____
4. We transfer money automatically into a savings or retirement account monthly.	_____	_____
5. We diversify our savings (and we know what that means).	_____	_____
6. We know about how much of our money goes to taxes.	_____	_____
7. We pay the full balance off on any credit cards we use monthly.	_____	_____
8. We know how much debt we have, if any.	_____	_____
9. We know how much savings we have at this moment.	_____	_____
10. We have an emergency fund that is at least or over $500 and we continue adding to it routinely.	_____	_____
11. We know how much we have to invest now to retire later in life.	_____	_____
12. When we want something expensive, we save for it and then buy it.	_____	_____
13. We have short-term and long-term financial goals in writing.	_____	_____
14. We have adequate insurance for our currently family situation.	_____	_____
15. We keep good financial records (e.g., bank statements, credit card bills and receipts, investment statements, tax forms, insurance policies).	_____	_____
16. We know how much is available to spend in our checking account.	_____	_____

	TRUE	FALSE

17. We check our individual credit reports annually.   _____   _____

18. We have up-to-date wills.   _____   _____

19. We pay extra on any loans we have (e.g., mortgage/car loans). _____   _____

20. We actually read financial statements sent to us and   _____   _____
understand what they are saying (e.g., banking, credit card,
mortgage, etc.).

SCORING:

Count up the number of Xs you have under the TRUE column.
Find your number below.

of TRUE Answers:

All 20   Congratulations, Mr. Buffett. You are financially
                          fit. Keep up the good work and stay on top of
                          things. There's always something new to learn.

15–19   You're in very good shape but review the
                          statements you answered as FALSE and see where
                          you can improve.

10–14   It wouldn't hurt you to pay a little more attention
                          to how you manage your money. In this case, the
                          truth hurts. Just a little. Get with the program.

9 or fewer   Dude. You need to learn how to manage your
                          money more effectively, and the sooner, the
                          better. Check out the recommended resources
                          in this chapter and commit to improvement.

TAKING YOUR FINANCIAL FITNESS TO A HIGHER LEVEL

You can up your own level of financial literacy with a little help from the cost-effective (read: free) resources around you.

Visit the Financial Readiness Program at the nearest family center on a military installation near you. They usually have a variety of classes and workshops available. You can also meet one-on-one with a financial readiness counselor and perhaps even a certified financial planner.

Access Military OneSource at www.militaryonesource.mil (Personal Financial Management and Taxes tab), and you will find many tools available to you free of charge, such as financial calculators and how-to articles covering the following topics:

- Budgeting basics
- Financial planning for deployment
- Protecting your financial health
- Savings tools
- Tax preparation and resources
- Financial planning

There is even a section on the Blended Retirement System with easy access to the opt-in course.

Military OneSource also offers you free financial counseling available in person, by phone, or by video-chat. Counselors are available online, or you can call 1-800-342-9647, and they can:

- Teach you how to talk to creditors to negotiate late fees and payment plans
- Help point you in the right direction if you are behind on your mortgage or facing foreclosure
- Help you figure out how to best save for college
- Discuss savings, retirement, and investment plans with you[22]

Take advantage of the massive amount of free financial education information and resources that trustworthy organizations make available to you. Here are great examples of such organizations:

- *The USAA Educational Foundation* offers access to Command Your Cash: Tools, tips, and tactics to help military service members develop sound financial habits and take control of their personal finances. (https://usaaef.org)
- *The Consumer Federation of America* offers access to Military Saves, a program dedicated to helping service members and their families save money, reduce debt, and build wealth. (https://militarysaves.org)
- *The FINRA Investor Education Foundation*'s SaveAndInvest.org is a free, unbiased resource dedicated to your financial health that offers easy-to-use tools and resources. SaveAndInvest.org helps you make informed financial decisions and arms you with the information you need to protect yourself from investment fraud. (https://www.saveandinvest.org/military)

And while they are in the financial education business per se, military relief societies can also provide assistance and information to service members and families who face emergency needs. Each branch of service has its own society:

- Army Emergency Relief (AER), https://www.aerhq.org/Apply-for-Assistance
- Air Force Aid Society (AFAS), https://www.afas.org
- Navy–Marine Corps Relief Society (NMCRS), http://www.nmcrs.org
- Coast Guard Mutual Assistance (CGMA), http://www.cgmahq.org

10 $MART MONEY MANAGEMENT TIPS

Tip #1: Create a Livable Spending Plan

Once upon a time they were called budgets. Now they are called spending plans, and you should have one. A spending plan gives you control over your finances. It's a snapshot telling you how much money you have coming in and where you are spending it. It also shows you where you can adjust your spending if need be. Anyone can create a spending plan easily.

The following steps from our friends at SaveAndInvest.org[23] have been adapted slightly for use here:

1. *Add up your monthly expenses.* Create a list showing what you pay out monthly. It might include such things as your mortgage/rent payment, car payment, insurance premiums, utilities, and phone bills.

2. *Add up your household's monthly take-home pay.* This includes after-tax pay for you and your spouse and any other income, such as investment or rental income. If you are retiring from the military, this category may include military retirement pay and any VA disability pay.

3. *Subtract your expenses from your income.* If the number isn't a pretty one, start looking for areas where you can cut back on your spending. Do you really need to have the premium cable package, Netflix, and iTunes? Can you limit your dining out?

4. *List your other financial priorities (e.g., an emergency fund, debt reduction, retirement savings, and/or college).* How much time do you need to reach that goal? Divide the time (in months) into the amount to find out how much you have to save monthly to reach it.

5. *Match your money with your expenses and your goals.* Make each dollar serve a purpose for you.

6. *Review and revise your plan each payday, or at least monthly.* Much like a resume, a spending plan is subject to change as life happens.

Tip #2: Track Your Spending

Setting up a spending plan is great, but it won't do you any good unless you track your spending correctly. You can track in a number of different ways:

- Carry a small notebook with you, and every time you spend money, write down the amount and what you spent it on.
- Use a free smartphone app such as Wallaby, Mint, Level Money, Dollarbird, or EveryDollar.
- Use your online banking export file feature to capture a range of dates in a particular account and save it to a spreadsheet.

It doesn't matter how you choose to do, as long as you do it.

Tip #3: Put Your Short- and Long-Term Financial Goals Down on Paper

Going through the motion of thinking about your goals, giving them actual words, and putting those words into full sentences on paper can make them more real to you. Goals, as you may already know, are far more effective when they are SMART:

S—specific

M—measurable

A—achievable

R—relevant

T—timely

An example of a SMART goal: I will build an emergency savings account by saving 10 percent of each paycheck I get until I reach $500.

Tip #4: Check Your Credit Report Annually

Each year, directed by federal law, you are entitled to one free credit report from each of the three major credit reporting agencies in the United States:

- TransUnion
- Experian
- Equifax

Free is the operative word here. *Directed by federal law* is the operative phrase. To access your free report, visit www.annualcreditreport.com. There are other websites out there that resemble this site, but they charge you for your report. Avoid them. Also bear in mind that even though your credit report is free, you may have to pay a small sum (usually under $15) to get your all-important FICO score.

Tip #5: Figure Out Your Net Worth

Your net worth is the value of all your assets less the total of all your liabilities. You can calculate your net worth using an online calculator (or you can create one yourself on paper easily enough).

Assets include:

Bank accounts (checking, savings, CDs, money markets)

Personal property (home, car[s], boats, collectibles, jewelry, and other belongings)

Investments (stocks, bonds, mutual funds, ETFs, real estate/REITs, life insurance, college savings plans)

Retirement savings (TSP, 401(k), 403(b), 457, SIMPLE, Keogh, IRAs, pension plans, annuities)

Money you're owed

Liabilities include:

Credit cards (what you owe on them)

Loans (mortgage, second mortgage or home equity loans, car loans, student loans, bank loans)

Investment loans (brokerage account loan, 401(k) loan, life insurance loan, business loan)

Back taxes or other debts owed

Simply add up your assets. Add up your liabilities. Subtract your liabilities from your assets, and voilà! You will then know what your net worth is at that moment in time.

Tip #6: Determine Whether You Have Adequate Life Insurance

If something bad happened to you, would your family struggle to make ends meet? Would they miss not only you but also your steady income? Could they afford to bury you or honor your last request and blast your ashes out of a cannon if need be? Do you have children who need to be supported while they are still growing up? Do they want to go to college one day? Does your spouse, working outside the home or not, also have adequate life insurance?

You can access http://www.lifehappens.org/insurance-overview/life-insurance/calculate-your-needs/, plug in the numbers, and see whether you're adequately covered. Easy.

Tip #7: Automate Savings, Investments, and Bill Paying

Paying yourself first, investing in your future, and paying your monthly bills automatically will save you the angst of being late and paying late fees for it. Check with your bank and find out just how easy it is to do this.

Tip #8: Use Credit Wisely

The concept of credit usually gets a bad rap, but credit used wisely isn't such a bad thing. For example, one day you may want to buy a house. Unless you have the cash on hand to buy that house, you're probably going to have to borrow the money from a bank. You will get infinitely better interest rates from that bank if you can show that you can be trusted with credit. The bank will check your credit report (see Tip #4), and that's how they will find out whether you are trustworthy. Your charming personality and cute smile just won't cut it here. So don't abuse credit, but use it wisely so, if need be, it can serve you later.

Tip #9: Think Ahead to Your Future Expenses and Save for Them Now

The water heater will eventually need replacing. Your kid is going to grow up and want to go to college. You will want to go on that European vacation for your big anniversary. These are expenses that you know will eventually show up on your doorstep. If you know they (or similar expenses) are coming, then start to set aside money for them now. You'll be ever so happy you did when the day comes to book your flight.

Tip #10: Consider Working with a Financial Planner

Not everyone is good at figuring out his finances, even with the plethora of freebie quality financial education out there. Even if you are good at it, getting trusted and objective professional financial guidance isn't a bad idea. Your needs change as your life stage changes, and sometimes it is worth shelling out a fee to get a second opinion.

If you want to work with a financial planner, FINRA (the people who know what to ask) suggest you ask these questions:[24]

- What experience do you have working with people like me?
- What professional licenses do you currently hold?
- Are you registered with FINRA, the SEC, or a state securities regulator? If so, for how long and in what capacity?
- Do you or your firm have an overarching investment philosophy? If so, what is it?
- What types of services or products do you offer?
- Are there any products or services you don't offer? Why?

- How do you get paid? Do you receive commissions on products I buy or sell? A percentage of the amount of my assets you manage? A flat fee? Any other method? What other fees and expenses do you charge?
- Can you provide me with any customer references?

A Crash Course Plus in the Blended Retirement System

Angelina Jolie and Brad Pitt.

Kim Kardashian and Kanye West.

Taylor Swift and [fill in the blank].

You and the military's new Blended Retirement System (BRS).

Some relationships just seem so complicated on the surface, right? They don't have to be, though. Once you sort through the rampant rumors and alarming headlines, things can often turn out to be pretty basic in nature.

While you may never know all the sordid details involving celebrity break-ups and makeups, you can and *should* know all the facts about the Blended Retirement System (BRS), especially if they affect you or service members who look to you for guidance. You should also know all the facts if you are a military community service provider charged with keeping our service members, veterans, and their families up to date on news that affects them.

The BRS is not as complicated as you may initially think. It is just new, and, like all things new, it may take a little time and effort to become familiarized with it.

One thing is certain with the BRS, however: If you are affected by it, then you must take an active role in the process of learning about it.

AN OVERVIEW OF THE BRS AND YOUR TRAINING OPTIONS

The Blended Retirement System, as it nearly goes without saying at this point, is the military's modernized retirement plan that changes, well, just about everything you used to know about the military's retirement system.

Spoiler alert: The new Blended Retirement System is not just for service members who make it to twenty years or more and retire. The BRS is for everybody, or it certainly will be beginning January 1, 2018.

Worried much?

Maybe you should be worried. You certainly wouldn't be alone if you were. A whopping 45 percent of service members report being worried that the DoD won't provide adequate training on the new system.[1] Thirty-eight percent report not feeling overly confident that they will receive the retirement benefits promised to them when they transition out of service.[2]

The BRS is, after all, a significant change to how the concept of retirement has been handled within the military for generations. Service members and their families want to know how this thing is going to work and they want to understand it, too.

With the BRS affecting about 2.2 million people,[3] you can bet that the DoD has been keenly interested in training up the masses. If you are actively serving now, you've probably already been inundated with information.

In a major effort to educate leaders and service members, the DoD crafted a four-phase training program:[4]

- *Phase I*: Train the leadership within the service branches. This began in June 2016.
- *Phase II*: Train the installation and command financial counselors. This began in January 2017.
- *Phase III*: Make "opt-in" training available for current service members. This began in January 2017.
- *Phase IV*: Ensure service members who join after January 2018 receive BRS training (a.k.a. accession training) during their first months of service. This will, of course, be ongoing.

The DoD has been firm in communicating the message that "while training will happen at all levels, the decision on whether to opt in belongs to the individual. Leaders will be informers of—not advocates for—the new system."[5] To that end, commanders across the services will encourage service members to prepare accordingly for retirement. They will remind eligible individuals about the existence of the mandatory opt-in course. They will be tasked with ensuring that service members are given the time they need to access retirement and financial management counseling.

Thankfully, leaders will also be responsible for encouraging service members to share the information about the BRS with their spouses and family members; as (then) DoD director of financial readiness Wayne Boswell said, "We know a lot of these decisions will be made around the dinner table, with families' input in terms of lifelong financial decisions."[6]

There. That's a nice reminder that this is a big-picture issue that doesn't just affect the service member. It affects the spouse and the family.

Make no mistake about it: The BRS is a new and big deal. For the most part, the DoD has done and continues to do a great job in rolling out this new system. A lot of truly caring and smart people have been slaving away behind the scenes to take it from abstract concept to concrete reality.

Strip away all the fancy online classes, the many informational briefings, the PowerPoint presentations ad nauseam, and high-speed glossy brochures, and this is the one thing you must remember if you are going to get through this mega, yet inevitable, change successfully:

> It is YOUR responsibility to learn as much as you possibly can about the BRS from the DoD and from other trusted sources.

If you have a choice in the matter of whether to opt in to the BRS or stay put with the legacy retirement system, then you must take the opt-in course before you make the decision. You can do this through JKO Online (https://jko.jten.mil) with or without a CAC-enabled card. You can also access the course through Military OneSource (www.militaryonesource.mil).

Unlike other seemingly endless and boring online military training modules, this one is well designed and as engaging as it can be given the low excitement factor of the topic. The syllabus of the course looks like this:

- Course Introduction
- Pre-Test

- Lesson 1: Opt-In Basics
- Lesson 2: The Importance of Lifelong Financial Literacy
- Lesson 3: Financial Planning Concepts and the TSP
- Lesson 4: Differences in the "High-3" System and the BRS
- Lesson 5: Important Factors to Consider
- Lesson 6: Tools and Resources
- Post-Test
- Completion

The talking heads selected for the production are interesting, engaging, and easy to relate to and do a decent job of drilling down a complicated topic.

You should also consider meeting with a financial counselor and/or educator on the nearest military installation to discuss your unique situation. This service will be free of charge for you, compliments of Uncle Sam.

Later in this chapter, you will also hear from some other financial experts, from outside the DoD, who offer up constructive comments.

And, of course, you should also talk things over with your significant other.

WHO IS AFFECTED BY THE BRS AND WHO ISN'T

- If you join the military on or after January 1, 2018, you are in the BRS. You don't have a choice.
- If you are already in the military as of December 31, 2017, you are grandfathered into the current retirement system. That means if you retire from the military at twenty years (or more) of service, you will receive your monthly retirement check for life based on the high-3 legacy system unless you are eligible for the BRS and opt in to it. If you meet certain eligibility requirements, however, you may be eligible to move over to the BRS.
- If you are serving on active duty with less than twelve years total service as of December 31, 2017, or if you are a reservist with fewer than 4,320 retirement points as of that same date, then you will be *eligible* to opt in to the BRS. You will be required to take mandatory opt-in training and make a decision one way or the other. You will have the calendar year, January 1, 2018, to December 31, 2018, to make that decision.
- No one—repeat, no one—will be automatically moved into the BRS. The BRS goes into effect on January 1, 2018, but you will have the whole year to decide whether you want to opt in to it.

- If, by chance, you happen to be someone who is coming back into the military after being out (a *reentrant*), then you will have the remainder of 2018 or, depending on when you return to service, thirty days to make the decision.
- If you are already retired from the military, the BRS doesn't apply to you at all.

> If you are someone with a choice in the matter, choose wisely. Once you have said you will opt in or stay with the legacy system, you are in it for the long haul.
>
> There is no going back and changing your decision at a later date.
>
> Your decision is irrevocable and that is final. *Literally.*

A LAST LOOK AT THE LEGACY MILITARY'S RETIREMENT SYSTEM

The BRS may be new, but it certainly doesn't reflect the first time that the DoD has revised the existing retirement system for service members who stay on active duty or serve in the reserves for a period of time (usually a minimum of twenty years).

Over the years, there have been changes made in the name of pay reform and efficiencies, which have resulted in basically four types of retirements:

- *Final pay*: Your retirement is based on your final basic pay. The multiplier used is 2.5 percent. Cost of living adjustments (COLA) is based on the Consumer Price Index (CPI).
- *High-36*: Your retirement is an average of your highest thirty-six months of basic pay. The multiplier used is 2.5 percent, and COLA is based on the CPI.
- *Career Status Bonus (CSB)/REDUX*: Your retirement is an average of your highest thirty-six months of basic pay with a reduction of 1 percent for each year short of thirty years. COLA is based on CPI minus 1 percent. At age sixty-two, retired pay is made to equal the high-36. At the time, the future multiplier is made equal to the high-36, and future COLA continues at the CPI minus 1 percent.
- *Disability*: Your retirement pay is based on either your final pay or high-36 as appropriate to your case. The multiplier is 2.5 percent for each year of service or the disability percentage assigned by the service at the time of retirement. COLA is based on the CPI, and disability pay may be partially or completely excluded from federal and/or state taxes.

There have also been instances when temporary early retirements were authorized for service members meeting specific conditions. For example, in the 1993–2001 Temporary Early Retirement Authority (TERA), you had to have served at least fifteen but less than twenty years of active service between 1993 and 2001. This program ended in September 2002 and cannot be used again unless approved by Congress.

There is also a Temporary Early Retirement Authority (TERA) (2012–2018) currently in existence. To retire under this authority, you have to have served at least fifteen but less than twenty years of active service. According to the Defense Finance and Accounting Service (DFAS), the opportunity to retire under TERA will end on December 31, 2018.[7] Once it expires, any future use will have to be approved by Congress.

Of course, as you should know if you serve in uniform, just because those possibilities of retiring early from service exist doesn't mean that you are granted them automatically.

When the bean counters determine your actual retired base pay under this legacy framework,[8] they use two methods. Those methods are the final pay method and the high-36 month average method.

The final pay method, according to military pay officials, establishes the retired pay base equal to final base pay.

The high-36 month average method is the average of the highest thirty-six months of basic pay divided by thirty-six. Usually, your high-3 (as it is also referred to) happens during your last three years of service.

The method used, however, depends on when you first entered the military. If you joined before September 8, 1980, you use the final pay method. If you joined on or after September 8, 1980, you use the high-36 method.

Each of the methods relies on the use of a 2.5 percent retirement multiplier to calculate retirement pay. The longer you serve, the higher your multiplier and the higher your retirement pay. (See table 2.1.)

Through the years after you retire, the cost of living goes up. Your retirement pay does as well, theoretically. The cost of living adjustment (COLA) is based on changes in the Consumer Price Index (CPI) as measured by the Department of Labor (DoL).[9]

Military retired pay is also subject to a dollar-for-dollar offset when the retired service member is receiving VA disability pay at the same time.[10]

Table 2.1. Legacy Military Retirement System Multipliers

Years of Service	10	15	20	21	22	23	24	25	30	35	40	41
Final Pay (%)	25	37.5	50	52.5	55	57.5	60	62.5	75	87.5	100	102.5
High-36 (%)	25	37.5	50	52.5	55	57.5	60	62.5	75	87.5	100	102.5
REDUX* (%)	n/a	n/a	40	43.5	47	50.5	54	57.5	75	87.5	100	102.5

*Multiplier does not apply to the REDUX retirement plan at under twenty years of service since REDUX is only an active-duty retirement plan.

FIVE BASIC POINTS TO KNOW ABOUT THE BRS

The U.S. Uniformed Services Blended Retirement System

Active Component

EFFECTIVE JANUARY 1 2018

Saving with the New Blended Retirement System

The Fiscal Year 2016 National Defense Authorization Act provides our military force with a modernized retirement plan built for retirement savings. Beginning in 2018, service members can get **automatic and matching Thrift Savings Plan contributions**, as well as a mid-career compensation incentive, in addition to **monthly retired pay for life.** All service members under the current system are grandfathered into today's retirement system, but some will be eligible to opt into the new Blended Retirement System.

Pre-2018 Retirement System:

Annuity

2.5% x Years Served x **Retired Pay Base**
after completing 20 years of service

Blended Retirement System Components

1 Automatic and Matching Contributions

Automatic contributions are seen immediately

You Contribute	DoD Auto Contribution	DoD Matches	Total
0%	1%	0%	1%
1%	1%	1%	3%
2%	1%	2%	5%
3%	1%	3%	7%
4%	1%	3.5%	8.5%
5%	1%	4%	10%

The DoD automatically contributes 1% of your basic pay to your **Thrift Savings Plan** after **60 days of service.**

You'll see matching contributions at the start of 3 years through the completion of 26 years of service, and...

You're fully vested—it's yours to keep—after completing 2 years of service and it goes with you when you leave.

2 Continuation Pay

Received at the mid-career point

You may receive a **cash payment** in exchange for additional service.

3 Full Retired Pay

Received after completing 20 years of service

2% x Years Served x Retired Pay Base

Calculate your **retired pay base** by averaging **the highest 36** months of basic pay.

You'll gain this monthly annuity for life after completing 20 years of service.

Your Retirement System

Options for Collecting Your Retired Pay

Full retired pay as a monthly annuity

or

Lump sum + Reduced retired pay as a monthly annuity

50% or 25% of monthly retired pay annuity bumps back up to 100% at full retirement age (67 in most cases).

If you joined the service or signed a contract to serve:

BEFORE January 1, 2006

You'll be grandfathered into the pre-2018 retirement system.

AFTER December 31, 2005 BUT BEFORE January 1, 2018

You'll have the choice to enroll in the Blended Retirement System or remain in the pre-2018 retirement system.

AFTER December 31, 2017

You'll be automatically enrolled in the Blended Retirement System.

You can find additional information at http://militarypay.defense.gov/BlendedRetirement
Sources: Sections 631, 632, 633, 634, and 635 of the Fiscal Year 2016 National Defense Authorization Act.

Revised. 9/2016

Source: Sections 631, 632, 633, 634, and 635 of the Fiscal Year 2016 National Defense Authorization Act

The U.S. Uniformed Services Blended Retirement System | *Reserve Component*

The Fiscal Year 2016 National Defense Authorization Act provides our military force with a modernized retirement plan built for retirement savings. Beginning in 2018, Reserve Component service members can get **automatic and matching Thrifts Savings Plan contributions, a mid-career compensation** incentive, and if they obtain 20 years of service, **monthly retired pay** for life starting at age 60.* All service members under the current system are grandfathered into today's retirement system.

Effective Date: January 1, 2018

Retirement System Selection

 Reserve Component members with more than 4,320 retirement points will remain under the legacy retirement system.

 Reserve Component members with less than 4,320 retirement points as of December 31, 2017, will have the choice of whether to opt into the new Blended Retirement System or remain in the legacy retirement system.

 New accessions after January 1, 2018, will automatically be enrolled in the new Blended Retirement System.

Reservists and Guardsmen While Serving

Thrift Savings Plan Contributions

You Contribute	DoD Auto Contribution	DoD Matches	Total
0%	1%	0%	1%
1%	1%	1%	3%
2%	1%	2%	5%
3%	1%	3%	7%
4%	1%	3.5%	8.5%
5%	1%	4%	10%

The DoD automatically contributes 1% of your basic pay or Inactive Duty Pay to your **Thrift Savings Plan** after **60 days of service.**

You'll see matching contributions at the start of 3 years through the completion of 26 years of service, and...

You're fully vested — it's yours to keep — after completing 2 years of service and it goes with you if you leave.

Continuation Pay
Received at the mid-career point

At the mid-career mark, you may receive a cash payment in exchange for additional service.

Retired Reservists and Guardsmen Eligible for Retirement Pay

Monthly Annuity for Life

2% x x

Years Served   Retired Pay Base

Calculate your **retired pay base** by averaging **the highest 36** months of basic pay.

You'll gain this monthly annuity for life after completing 20 qualifying years of service and attaining age 60*

*or earlier based on qualifying active service.

Collecting Your Retired Pay

OPTION 1 Full retired pay annuity beginning at age 60 or earlier based on credited active service

or

OPTION 2 Lump sum   with   Reduced retired pay as monthly annuity

25% or 50% lump sum and reduced monthly annuity at age 60 Monthly annuity bumps back up to 100% at full retirement age (67 in most cases).*

You can find additional information at http://militarypay.defense.gov/BlendedRetirement
Sources: Fiscal Year 2016 National Defense Authorization Act, sections 631,632, 634, and 635

> **Basic Point #1**
> The BRS offers variety.

The BRS "blends" elements from the legacy retirement system with government automatic and matching contributions to the Thrift Savings Plan (TSP). It offers a defined benefit, a defined contribution, and a continuation pay.

The legacy retirement plan is a defined pension plan. This change in semantics means that you are going to have to cough up more dough yourself if you want to experience a comfortable life in your old age.

In a defined contribution plan, a big piece of the BRS for the majority of participants, you fund your own retirement. The government, in this case, will assist by providing some matching funds. (More on that in Point #3.) Civilians who work outside the government are already used to this if they work for an employer that offers a 401(k) or similar investment vehicle.

> **Basic Point #2**
> If you retire from the military, then you will still get an annuity (albeit a smaller one), and you will have the option to elect a lump sum payment, too.

With the BRS, the basic qualifications for a military retirement do not change. You still have to meet the requirements to retire from service, and when you do, you will receive the traditional defined benefit annuity (a.k.a. the monthly retirement paycheck). While those automatic deposits are nice to see pop up in your bank account on a regular basis, you should know they will be 20 percent less than they would have been under the legacy system. The BRS adjusts the years of service multiplier from 2.5 percent (what is used in the old retirement system) to 2.0 percent for the purpose of calculating monthly retirement pay.

What does that mean in terms of real numbers? Let's look at an example.

Let us assume you are retiring from service after twenty years. (Congratulations, by the way.) If you fall under the legacy system, your gross (before taxes) monthly retirement paycheck would be $2,103. The multiplier is 2.5 percent. The number of years in service is twenty. When you multiply those two numbers, you get 50 percent, meaning your retirement pay would be 50 percent of the average of your high-3. Your high-3 average is $4,205, and 50 percent (or half) of that is $2,103.

Legacy Retirement
2.5 x 20 = 50%
$4,205.00 x 50% = $2,103.00

If you opted into the BRS, however, the numbers will look different.

BRS Retirement
2.0 x 20 = 40%
$4,205.00 x 40% = $1,682.00

About the Lump Sum Option

There is also a new option with the BRS for those who retire from the military. When you are ninety days from retirement, you may choose to receive a lump sum payment of 50 percent or 25 percent of the *discounted present value* of your future retirement payments.

If the phrase *discounted present value* is confusing to you, it's understandable. The DoD supposedly determines this amount by estimating what your retired pay will be and then reducing it to its value in "today's dollars" by using a formula based on many factors, including market conditions.[11]

If you elect to do this, your monthly annuity (your retirement check) will only be 50 percent or 75 percent (depending on your election) of what you would have otherwise received. When you grow older and reach Social Security's definition of "full retirement age," which for most people is the ripe old age of sixty-seven, you will begin getting bigger monthly retirement paychecks, as it will then revert back to being a full annuity.

Reserve component (RC) service members also have the option of electing a lump sum payment of retired pay. According to the DoD, however, RC members qualifying for a "non-regular retirement" are not eligible to get this lump sum until becoming eligible for retired pay, usually at sixty years of age. Age of eligibility may be reduced, however, if you have certain types of qualifying service.[12]

Taxing Matters of the Lump Sum Option

Retirement pay is subject to taxation, and the lump sum payment you might elect at retirement is no exception. Taxes, much like death, are forever.

You can minimize the potential tax liability by taking your lump sum in installments over several years (a maximum of four installments, one per year).[13] Consult with a trusted tax advisor before you make a final decision.

Finally, if you are going to be a military retiree who will receive a disability rating from the Department of Veterans Affairs (VA), then understand now that any disability compensation due to you could be affected or delayed if you choose the lump sum option.[14]

Basic Point #3
You could save big with the Thrift Savings Plan IF you are disciplined enough to do so. (Hint: You need to be disciplined enough.)

The Thrift Savings Plan (TSP) is a defined contribution plan that is available to those who work for the U.S. government. It is a long-term retirement savings and investment plan much like the 401(k) plans that employers outside of the government offer to their employees. If you are currently serving, you may even already contribute to the TSP, although the government isn't matching your contributions.

The 1 Percent Government Contribution to Your TSP

With the BRS, the government will automatically contribute an amount equal to an additional 1 percent of your basic pay to your TSP account. You don't have to contribute anything, and it will still do this. It won't, however, match its own 1 percent amount here.

You Have to Contribute Cash, Too

The whole point of having a TSP is to create wealth for long-term savings. In other words, you have to put up some cash if you want it to grow.

Based on your TSP contribution, you can receive a government-matching contribution up to 4 percent of your basic pay for a total of 5 percent government contribution to your TSP. (See table 2.2.)

Table 2.2. TSP: Government Matches

You Contribute (%)	Government Automatic Contribution (%)	Government Matches (%)	Total (%)
0	1	0	1
1	1	1	3
2	1	2	5
3	1	3	7
4	1	3.5	8.5
5	1	4	10

Source: DoD BRS Opt-In Training Course

Of course, that concept of "up to additional 4 percent" means that you have to ante up "up to additional 4 percent" of your pay as well. They won't just give it to you because you look cute in uniform.

In other words, you will have to give up more of your current pay now to theoretically see adequate retirement results later in life.

Remember, while the DoD wants to see more of those who serve in uniform get something financially out of their service over the long haul, whether they retire from the military or not, they also want to save money. They'll match, but you have to give it up, too.

Government-matching contributions will continue to be for you as long as you continue contributing and until you separate from service, retire from service, or complete twenty-six years of service.[15]

Deductions for your contributions can be made automatically from your paycheck, and you have a choice regarding whether you want your contributions to be pretax (traditional) or after tax (Roth). Consult with a tax advisor to see which path is best for you.

You should also be aware that the TSP offers low administrative and investment expenses. In 2016, the TSP management fee was .03 percent per year.

Under certain circumstances, you may be able to access your TSP funds while you are still in uniform. And, of course, you get to say who gets the money should you die before you can enjoy it yourself.

About Vesting

Vesting is all about when you get to keep your money in the TSP. It refers to the time-in-service requirement that you must meet before you're entitled to keep your earnings.

You are fully vested in your own contributions and earnings, as well as any matching contributions (if any), from the first day you contribute.

The 1 percent contribution that the government makes to your TSP in the BRS, however, is different. You have to serve at least two years before that becomes yours to take with you when you transition out. According to the DoD, all service counts toward vesting, not just service as a TSP participant.[16] If you leave service before two years, then you forfeit your government 1 percent contributions and their earnings. If you die before leaving the military, however, then your beneficiaries are automatically considered vested in all of the money in your account.

According to the DoD, if you are serving in a combat zone, you can contribute tax-exempt pay to your traditional TSP account or to your Roth account. If you contribute tax-exempt pay to your traditional account, the amount you contribute will be tax-free when you withdraw it. If you contribute tax-exempt pay to a Roth account, both the amount contributed and its earnings will be tax-free when you withdraw them, assuming you have satisfied the regular Roth withdrawal requirements.[17]

When You Leave the Military

When you retire or transition out of service, the TSP is still yours to do with what you will, and you do have options.

- You can do nothing and let it sit right where it is. It will continue to grow tax deferred until you start taking money out of it. You won't be able to contribute to it, however.
- You can roll it over to an Individual Retirement Account (IRA) or to a qualified employer plan.
- You can cash it out, but expect to pay a significant early withdrawal penalty and federal income tax as well.

There may be other options here, too. Suffice it to say that when the time comes for you to leave the military, whether you are retiring out of it or simply transitioning out of it, know that your funds can go with you. Consider consulting with a financial planner, and always read the fine print on the www.TSP.gov website carefully.

Basic Point #4
Continuation pay = a convincing carrot to complete the journey.

In addition to the new features of the TSP, the DoD offers eligibility for continuation pay. It might have made more sense had they just called this what it seems to be—a bonus pay.

Continuation pay, a direct cash payout, was included within the framework of this new system to encourage service members to continue serving for four more years in uniform once they reach that *Do I stay or do I go?* point in their careers.

While it is not considered part of the retirement benefit, it is something the DoD deems essential in the effort to maintain retention rates of skilled individuals, as they surmise that fewer service members will stay until retirement without the legacy system.[18]

How much continuation pay you might receive depends on the career field you are working in and how important the DoD feels it is to keep you, a skilled and experienced expert, in that job, in uniform.

The amounts paid for service in each career field can vary from year to year, but they will always be in the range of a minimum of 2.5 months of basic pay up to a maximum of thirteen months of basic pay for an active component member and a minimum of 0.5 months of basic pay up to a maximum of six months of basic pay for a reserve component member.[19] Active guard/reserve and full-time support members will be paid at least the minimum of 2.5 months of basic pay if they are serving on active duty.[20]

The DoD points out that some members of the reserve component may fall into a gray area. They will be eligible to opt in to the BRS because they have less than 4,320 points, but they will be past the twelve-year point in their careers. These individuals will be eligible to opt in to the BRS, but they will not be eligible for continuation pay.[21]

> **Basic Point #5**
> You have resources available to help you weigh the decision to opt in.

Retirement pay. Lump sum pay. TSP contributions. Continuation pay.

There are so many moving pieces to the BRS, aren't there? All you want to do is make the right decision for you and your family. You're not even sure what that is, even after reading all this terrific (and very well-written, thank you) information.

Relax. You're on a journey for enlightenment, grasshopper. This is but one step, and there are other resources you can access to help move you further along in the decision-making process.

The much-anticipated BRS Comparison Calculator (in beta form as of May 4, 2017) is available at http://militarypay.defense.gov/Calculators/BRS/. Use it. If you want an overview of how to use it, revisit the mandatory BRS opt-in training online. The last lesson of the course does a great job of explaining how it works and what kind of information you need to input in order to run good numbers.

COMMONLY ASKED QUESTIONS AND ANSWERS ABOUT THE BRS[22]

Question #1: Is the BRS a good thing for me and my family?

Good is always relative. The BRS is good in that it will touch a majority of those who serve, whereas only those who made it to twenty years would benefit before. Even if you don't retire from the military, when you leave, you leave with something. Yay you. If you stay for your full twenty years or more and retire from the military, you still get a monthly retirement check and even the option to take a lump sump at retirement (at the expense of lowering your monthly retirement check, of course, and potentially paying significant taxes on that lump sum unless you structure a disbursement over time).

Will it be as good or better than the legacy retirement system, if you are a lifer? Will it be good for you if you aren't a lifer? That depends solely on you. Remember, good is relative. If you are eligible for and elect to participate in the BRS, then its success will largely depend on whether you sacrifice a portion of your paycheck now for later. You're going to have to be a good saver within the TSP. If you're not, then you won't enjoy the potential benefits of this system.

Question #2: I think I'm eligible for the BRS. What do I have to do?

First of all, don't *think* you're eligible for the BRS. *Know* whether you are. Review "Who Is Affected by the BRS and Who Isn't" above and figure out the right answer. If you are indeed eligible to participate in the BRS, then you'll be required to complete the opt-in training course. See "An Overview of the BRS and Your Training Options" above to learn how to take that required training.

Question #3: I am eligible for the BRS. I completed the required training. I don't want to participate in the BRS. What do I do now?

If you serve in the U.S. Army, U.S. Air Force, or U.S. Navy and want to remain under the legacy retirement system, your next step is easy: Do nothing. Nada. Zilch. Nichts.

If you are a U.S. Marine or serve with the U.S. Public Health Service Commissioned Corps or in the National Oceanic and Atmospheric Administration Commissioned Officer Corps, then be on the lookout for further guidance from your command. Do not stress, however. You won't be automatically moved into the BRS. No one will. Those who are eligible must intentionally opt in to be a part of it.

Question #4: I am eligible for the BRS and I want to opt in. How do I do it?

If you are in the U.S. Army, U.S. Navy, or U.S. Air Force, you simply click and opt. Log on to your MyPay account at the Defense Finance and Accounting Service (DFAS) website and follow the direction to opt in. If you don't have a MyPay account, you should probably get one. If you have questions, consult with your chain of command or your personnel office.

If you are a U.S. Marine, you can opt in at Marine OnLine.

If you serve with the U.S. Public Health Service Commissioned Corps or in the National Oceanic and Atmospheric Administration Commissioned Officer Corps, then be on the lookout for further guidance from your command.

Question #5: I heard that I have the whole year of 2018 to decide whether to opt in to the BRS if I want to do so. If I opt in, does it matter when?

If you opt in sooner, you begin receiving automatic and matching government contributions sooner, specifically on the first effective pay date after you opt in. That means the sooner you commit and start aggressively saving, the more you benefit. That said, don't rush the decision. Make sure you get all your questions answered first, and yes, you have until December 31, 2018, to do that.

Question #6: Can I try it before I buy into it?

Sorry. Nope. You get one shot here. Either you go for it or you don't. Once you've made that decision, that's it. There is no going back.

Question #7: What if I have a break in service? Can I still opt into the BRS?

Yes. No worries. If you have left or leave the military and you rejoin after the opt-in decision year of 2018, then you will have thirty days to decide whether to stay in the legacy retirement system or go for the BRS, so long as you meet eligibility requirements.

WHAT TRUSTED EXPERTS (OUTSIDE THE DOD) ARE SAYING

If you have a choice of whether to buy into the BRS, should you? While it would make it infinitely easier to have someone make that decision for you, that just isn't going to happen. Only you can decide whether the BRS is the right choice for you and your family.

Theoretically, you have a good understanding of your own financial situation. The DoD will not tell you what to do. You can see why, under these circumstances, it's important for you to get as smart as you can on the topic.

In the course of educating yourself, it may also be beneficial to hear what others have to say about it. Specifically, others who have expertise on all things financial.

Before you make up your mind about the BRS, take advantage of the ability to access financial counselors and educators on your military installation.

It won't hurt to hear what others who work away from the installation say, too. On that note, we've asked five trusted experts their thoughts on the BRS.

Here is what they had to say. . . .

Joseph "J. J." Montanaro, CFP
Relationship Director, Military Advocacy Group
USAA

Mr. Montanaro is a certified financial planner with more than twenty years of experience working in the financial services industry. He is a registered investment advisor and a member of the Financial Planning Association. He is a graduate of the United States Military Academy, West Point, New York, where he earned his bachelor's degree in engineering. Before entering the financial services industry, he served in the U.S. Army for six years on active duty, and in 2009 he retired as a lieutenant colonel in the United States Army Reserve. His advice has appeared in numerous outlets, including the Wall Street Journal, USA Today, *CNNMoney.com, MarketWatch.com,* Military Spouse Magazine, *and the* Washington Post. *He hosts USAA's* Money Drill *podcast.*

The vast majority of those that serve don't qualify for retirement benefits and the new Blended Retirement System will change that. For the first time, the DoD will add money to service members' TSP accounts. That's pretty cool.

On the whole, I'm excited about the possibilities that the BRS creates. It's definitely going to touch a lot more service members than the current system.

My hope is that BRS will be a change agent, ultimately causing millions of young service members to start saving for the future. TSP participation in the uniformed services plan has hovered around 40 percent for years and this, I hope, will drive that number way up.

If you ultimately retire from the military, the new system will probably mean less in terms of DoD-provided retirement benefits, but you can help fill that gap by taking advantage of the TSP.

No matter where someone falls as far as the BRS is concerned, I think all service members should strongly consider participating in the TSP. . . . It's a great way to build for the future.

When it comes to deciding between the BRS and the High-3 system, the key question, which no one can answer definitively, is whether or not you're going to serve 20 years and retire. Personal and career goals, health, family situation and, yes, the needs of the service, all factor into how long someone serves.

While I can't tell you BRS or High-3, I can tell you definitively that making the TSP a part of your financial routine is a great way to build for the future.

If you choose the BRS or enter the service after 2018 and it's your retirement plan, there's one must, and that's to contribute at least 5 percent to the TSP to get the full match from the DoD.

Let's not forget that even with BRS, the monthly military retirement check is not going away. Yes, it's getting a not insignificant 20 percent haircut, but if you survey the benefits landscape, there are fewer and fewer pensions out there, so the BRS monthly annuity is still a beautiful thing.

Shane Ostrom, CFP
Deputy Director, Finance and Benefits Information
Military Officers Association of America

Mr. Ostrom retired from the U.S. Air Force in 2000 after serving in a variety of personnel, education and training, and executive officer assignments. His assignments included tours in North Dakota, Florida, Korea, Australia, and the

Pentagon. His final assignment was on the Joint Staff, writing and champion-
ing legislation related to joint officer personnel management issues. He earned
numerous decorations and awards over his military career.

After retiring from the U.S. Air Force, Mr. Ostrom was a practicing invest-
ment advisor at a large investment firm and a bank. He specialized in working
with clients developing, implementing, and managing investment plans and
portfolios. A native of San Antonio, Texas, he earned a bachelor of arts and
master of arts and is a graduate of the Royal Australian Air Command and
Staff College and the U.S. Air Command and Staff College.

Mr. Ostrom joined the MOAA staff in 2006. His responsibilities include
researching and writing articles and answering member inquiries regarding
military benefits, health care, survivor issues, and financial concerns. He also
travels extensively to discuss these matters with service members and retirees
and their families.

Let me start at the bottom line and explain my position afterwards. If you are
sure you will serve until retirement or if you are not sure whether you will serve
to retirement, stay with the current retirement program. If you are absolutely,
100 percent sure you are getting out prior to retirement, take the new retirement program.

For those of you who are not sure, welcome to the club.

I'm willing to bet a large number of retirees did not originally expect to stay
in and retire. Me included.

If you go with the new retirement program thinking you will get out and you
don't, boy will you have buyers' remorse.

The data on the status of retirement savings in America is shocking; we are
not saving enough and we are not good investors. This after 401ks have been
around since 1978. Too many people will find themselves living at a lower
living standard in retirement or working for much longer than they planned.

Pensions are incredibly important for most people—yet pensions are dis-
appearing. Well, you say, I'll still have a pension under the new retirement
program. Yeah, but 20% less to start, 20% less figuring future cost of living
increases and over a lifetime that means you are giving up huge lifetime
earnings.

Can you accumulate wealth using a TSP with a match? You betcha, IF you
contribute enough and you have an investment strategy that works. But again,
the almost 40 years of national data suggest otherwise.

Go with the current pension and accumulate wealth at the same time in the TSP or other investment vehicles. The match is nice but not more meaningful than the pension. Do you seriously think the government decreased the pension to establish a match because the match is better for Service members?

What about all of you with no choice?

If you are locked into the current plan, great. You'll have nice lifetime, cost of living adjusted income plus your investments.

Learn how to be a good investor—it doesn't involve guesswork, predictions, trading, media or gambling. Read the MOAA web site (www.moaa.org) by selecting "Blog" under the "Publications and Media" header. Once in the Blog section screen, click on the category of Military Benefits and then select the subcategory of Finance. We are a source of unbiased information for your planning needs.

For those of you who will be locked into the new plan, you better learn how to be a good investor. Your financial future depends on it and the sooner you start, the better. Proper investing is a snowball rolling down a mountainside. The younger you are the taller your mountain.

Starlett Henderson, Accredited Financial Counselor
Veteran and Family Member Employment Specialist

Starlett Henderson is an accredited financial counselor and employment specialist for our U.S. military affiliated—veterans and family members. These particular callings are a result of her own military affiliations as a U.S. Army veteran and a longtime spouse of an active-duty, U.S. Army National Guard service member. Mrs. Henderson is a retired cofounder of Army Wife Network (AWN) and cohost of AWN's Army Wife Talk Radio, *the original Internet talk radio show designed specifically for military spouses. She is a coauthor of* 1001 Things to Love About Military Life *and has devotionals and stories published in award-winning books such as* Stories of Strength and Courage from the Wars in Iraq and Afghanistan *and* Stories Around the Table.

She is currently adjusting to her husband's newest duty station in Military City, USA (a.k.a. San Antonio, Texas), with her husband and their youngest child. They are figuring out day hiking, road trips, and everything outdoors, in the heat. But at least "it's a dry heat!"

When it comes to the National Defense Authorization Act (NDAA)'s forthcoming Blended Retirement System (BRS), service members are in one of three groups.

- Those who will enter into service on the day BRS enters the scene (January 1, 2018) or after. BRS will be their retirement system.
- Those eligible to make a choice between the legacy "High 3" and the new Blended Retirement System during the 2018 calendar year.
- Those under the legacy "High 3" retirement system that will not be eligible to opt in to BRS. That includes my husband and, by association, our family.

To the service member who doesn't have a choice and has to go with the NEW system no matter what.

The DOD is giving you something many service members have been asking for [for] decades: a modernized retirement system that provides value early in their career, is portable and is somewhat self-directed. The Thrift Savings Plan (TSP), the defined contribution component of the BRS, fulfills those requests.

During my financial counseling fellowship at an army base, I learned of the paltry percentage of service members who participated in the TSP when it was a purely optional, investment offering. There were no explanations other than they did not know the value they were being offered and they perceived they couldn't afford to contribute. I can't speak to everyone's financial situation and beliefs about what they can or cannot afford, but I can attest that the value is beyond compare, namely where expenses are concerned. Now the military will be contributing on your behalf and then incentivizing your participation through matching contributions after two years of completed service.

This will not be "the old military way." You have a different set of basics under which you will operate. Veterans in your family and others who have served may not understand the new arrangement. They may assume something that is no longer true in regards to military retirement. You must arm yourself with the answers to many questions and avail yourself of all the tools that will aid you in maximizing this new way.

To the service member who does have a choice: the BRS or the legacy "High-3" system. What should you do?

You will have to get in the weeds with training and calculating to determine if you should actually opt-in to the blended retirement system. It is not the appropriate decision for everyone.

From where they are in their career to the planned number of years of service and from one's savings discipline to desired retirement goals and lifestyle, everyone's story varies. That is why financial counselors like me won't advise you or make this personal decision for you. Don't worry though. Educators and leaders will have access to the best resources needed to inform and support all the service members to make the choice with confidence and maximize their benefit.

Ask for time and access to the BRS calculator so you can visualize the difference in the growth of your savings between the systems. This exercise will provide data for the most informed decision on which plan to choose. You could come out the same or better, but you won't know without completing the mandatory opt-in BRS course and running YOUR numbers.

To the service member who doesn't have a choice and has to go with the OLD system no matter what.

Our family is in the third group. We made the personal decision to blend our retirement system before the BRS was (or will be) a thing.

I served eight years in the military. I planned to serve 20 years and receive the ultimate guaranteed benefit, a traditional military pension. Plans changed, and I separated from the military literally weeks before the TSP opened enrollment to uniformed service members. However, I took a federal job right out of the military where I learned about the TSP complete with matching contributions. I only stayed long enough to become vested, but I grew my TSP account to larger than I grew my IRA in the previous ten years.

At the same time, my husband transitioned from part-time to AGR (full-time) National Guard and began his TSP savings. He contributes still, fifteen years later. Competent financial educators and leaders have always encouraged us to provide for our own retirement by investing our own money outside government programs to supplement our promised retirement benefits. Some call it diversifying. For the purpose of this vignette, I'll call it blending responsibly.

No matter the system you choose or receive, please talk to individuals who can educate you on the pros and cons, point you to the resources you need, and inspire you to utilize your program to the maximum you can afford.

Doug Nordman, U.S. Navy (Retired)
Author, *The Military Guide to Financial Independence and Retirement*

Mr. Nordman is the author of The Military Guide to Financial Independence and Retirement *and* The Military Financial Independence and Retirement Pocket Guide. *He retired from the U.S. Navy after serving twenty years in the submarine force. He earned his bachelor's degree in chemistry from the U.S. Naval Academy.*

Mastering the management of his own financial situation has led him to achieve true financial independence. He and his retired navy spouse now enjoy a lovely life in Hawaii doing the things they enjoy, such as surfing, reading, studying the martial arts, and conducting home improvement projects. All of Mr. Nordman's income from his writing is donated to military charities.

First, who's eligible?

You're eligible to choose the Blended Retirement System if you started active duty after 2005. That means you should have less than 12 years of service before 2018.

You're eligible if you're in the Reserves or National Guard at the end of 2017 and will have fewer than 4,320 points (fewer than 12 years of retirement points) before 2018.

Anyone who enters the military before 2018 can stay with the existing High Three retirement system. That includes midshipmen and cadets at service academies, but ROTC students without prior service must have signed an agreement to serve as a commissioned officer.

Next, should you switch?

You should probably switch to the Blended Retirement System for its matching contributions to your Thrift Savings Plan, but you'll have to be financially responsible by maximizing those matching contributions. You're maximizing your TSP contributions now, right?

If you already know that you'll be on active duty for at least 20 years, then stick with the current High Three retirement. Be aware that the odds of reaching 20 are against you. Over 80% of today's service members—even those in the Reserves and National Guard—will leave the military before reaching retirement. They'll have only the money in their Thrift Savings Plan accounts and their personal savings. They won't be eligible for any military pension or matching funds.

If you leave active duty before 20 and complete your career in the Reserves or Guard, then your military pension starts at age 60. It'll be a smaller pension than active duty and it'll be delayed by as long as two decades after you apply for retirement. The amount of the Reserve/Guard pension won't be much different between the High Three or Blended Retirement Systems. However, if you've chosen the BRS and maximized your matching TSP contributions, then that investment will compound for the entire time until you start your pension. If those matching contributions are compounding in the TSP's L2050 fund then you might be ahead of the High Three pension.

You should only stay for 20 years of active duty if you're challenged and fulfilled. Maybe you've accepted a service obligation for medical school or pilot training that will take you to 20 years. But no matter what date you entered the military, by the time you reach 15 years your options are in the upper part of the career pyramid. You might be expected to do more leading and less operating. It could be difficult to get a good duty location or an interesting billet. You might be asked to take a hardship tour or move your family at a bad time. You might even be expected to "break out from the pack" by taking orders to the Pentagon or another large staff.

It's tempting to suck it up and gut it out on active duty for 20. You might be able to do that for two or three years. But if you're eligible for the Blended Retirement System then you're already facing at least eight more years of service. If you grimly clench your jaw and try to endure that extended misery on active duty then you're risking your physical, emotional, and even mental health. (Your family and friends will avoid you too.) Nobody should have to suffer that long for a military billet. You have far more ability (and human capital) than that, and you can find a different career that makes life worth living.

If you're pretty sure that you're leaving active duty before 20 years then take the Blended Retirement System. You won't earn an active-duty pension (neither will 80 percent of today's service members) but you'll take your matching TSP contributions with you. Those matching contributions will keep compounding for your retirement while you're figuring out your bridge career.

If you're maximizing your TSP and IRA contributions, and investing even more money in taxable accounts, then you might reach financial independence even without a military pension.

What if you don't have a choice?

If you're so senior that you have to stick with the current High Three pension system, then keep maximizing your contributions to your TSP and your IRA. Try to save even more in taxable accounts. If you leave active duty before you reach 20 years then you might still be able to qualify for a Reserve/Guard pension. Otherwise that's all the retirement investments you'll have.

If you join the military after 2017 then you'll be automatically enrolled in the TSP with a default contribution from your pay. After you complete your initial training and start learning your job, try to boost your TSP contributions as much as you can. Your next financial goal is to contribute enough to the TSP to earn all of the DoD match. After you reach that goal then you can start contributing to your IRA and then attempt to reach the maximum TSP contribution limit. Try to save even more in taxable accounts. Raise your TSP contribution with every pay raise and each promotion, and within 2–3 years you should be able to reach the limits.

If you can save at least 40 percent of your pay each year for up to 20 years, and invest in the TSP's L2050 fund or similar passively managed equity index funds, then you'll reach financial independence even without a military pension! You might decide to stay on active duty until 20, or choose to transfer to the Reserve/Guard, but your high savings rate will give you plenty of other life choices.

Attiyya S. Ingram, Accredited Financial Counselor
Ingram Financial Management

Mrs. Ingram is an accredited financial counselor who owns and operates Ingram Financial Management. A native of Philadelphia, Pennsylvania, she graduated, with honors, from Hampton University with a bachelor of science degree in accounting.

She found her passion for helping others gain control of their financial well-being when she began volunteering with the Navy–Marine Corps Relief Society. She continued volunteering her time by facilitating Dave Ramsey's Financial Peace University. During this same time she expanded her financial education by attending Boston University and earning a graduate certificate in financial planning. As a committed community servant, she also volunteered her financial management expertise at Volunteer Income Tax Assistance (VITA) offices as an Internal Revenue Service registered tax preparer.

In 2011, she was selected as a Financial Industry Regulatory Authority (FINRA) Military Spouse Fellow. This coveted fellowship authorized her to intern with the Army Community Service's Financial Readiness office, further contributing to the financial health of her military community. In 2012, she successfully completed the fellowship and was designated an Accredited Financial Counselor (AFC).

Currently, Mrs. Ingram works with multiple government contractors, providing financial counseling and education to members of our military and their families.

She began Ingram Financial Management in 2011 to provide trusted financial education and counseling, as well as income tax preparation services. She has successfully completed all paid tax preparer requirements set forth by the IRS.

Mrs. Ingram understands the challenges and rewards of military life as she is also the spouse of an active-duty U.S. Marine.

Created by the Fiscal Year 2016 National Defense Authorization Act, the new Blended Retirement System (BRS) combines the popular military retirement pension with an employer matching program found in most civilian defined contribution plans.

All participants receive an automatic 1 percent contribution and the Department of Defense (DoD) will match up to 4 percent of the individual's contribution. All DoD contributions will be placed in the traditional Thrift Savings Plan (TSP) and will be subject to income taxes when withdrawn.

The vast majority of service members leave the military before reaching the 20-year mark required to receive a pension and roughly 84 percent of service members do not participate in the TSP. This means, under the legacy system, most people leave military service without any retirement savings. The BRS will allow this majority to leave the military with a small balance in their TSP account.

Let's look at a couple specific examples:

Example one: Sean is an E-2 who has opted into the BRS. He's planning to separate from the military after four years of service and he is not making individual contributions to his TSP. However, because he made the BRS election he will receive a 1% DoD automatic contribution. When he exits the service, he will have roughly $1,000 in his TSP account.

Since the DoD is offering matching funds, also known as "free money," to service members throughout their career, they have reduced the retirement pension calculation. Currently, your monthly pension is calculated at 2.5 percent × the number of years you served × the average of your highest 36 months of base pay. With the BRS, your pension is calculated at 2.0% × the number of years you served × the average of your highest 36 months of base pay.

Example two: Ryan is an E-7 who is retiring after 20 years of active duty service under the legacy system. Under this system, he will receive roughly $2,283 a month (2.5% × 20 × $4,566). If, however, Ryan were to retire under the new BRS, he will receive roughly $1,826 a month (2.0% × 20 × $4,566).[23]

According to the Center for Disease Control, average life expectancy is age 78.8.[24] This means service members who enlist at age 18 and retire from the military at age 38, can expect to receive their military pension for 40 years. In the example above, when Ryan participates in the BRS, his pension is reduced by $456 per month. That's $5,472 per year, and $218,880 over 40 years (not including adjustments for the cost of living). Unless Ryan has taken advantage of the full DoD contribution of 5 percent per month over his 20-year career, his TSP balance will not be enough to offset his pension reduction. In addition, individuals cannot withdraw funds, penalty free, from their TSP until age 59½.

Careful consideration should be taken regarding how you will supplement this pension reduction in the years between your military retirement and when TSP withdraws can begin. Take the time to meet with an installation approved financial counselor/educator to gain a better understanding of your options.

II

MOVING FROM WHERE YOU ARE TO WHERE YOU WANT TO BE

3

The Space in Between Worlds

Everyone who joins the military eventually leaves the military. Either they transition out after a certain period of time or they retire after serving what seems like a lifetime in uniform.

No matter how you arrive at the military-to-civilian life transition crossroads, whether it is by carefully calculated design or by fate's cruel hands, accept that you have your work cut out for you on many levels.

Even if you plan carefully for your transition, do not expect the journey to be smooth sailing all the way. You can expect less-than-clear weather ahead. You may have to adjust your sails at some point.

No worries.

You are already trained to handle the contingencies.

GETTING YOUR HEART, MIND, AND FAMILY ON BOARD FOR THE JOURNEY

Transitioning out, whether you welcome it or not, can be an emotionally draining and stressful time period in your career and in your life.

If you have a family, they won't be unaffected, either.

To minimize potential heartache and poor decision making on what could be a grand scale, think carefully before you start making big life-altering decisions.

First, take the time to get your heart, your mind, and your family (if that applies to you) in sync in the beginning of this whole process. It will pay great dividends to do so.

One way to start doing that is to begin managing the expectations.

You May Be in for a Roller-Coaster Ride

As you take up residency in the netherworld of your new reality, still in uniform but with one foot out the door, expect to experience conflicting emotions.

One minute you might tingle with excitement over the prospect of this new life adventure that awaits you, while the next minute you find yourself terrified, physically shaking and curled up in the fetal position in the corner of a dark room.

Anxiety could become your little friend, and she may visit you often.

It is understandable to feel this way. Stress is an all too common side effect of change. You may be able to better manage transition stress when it happens if you plan preemptive strategies for dealing with it in advance.

File the following suggestions, adapted from the stress experts at WebMD, away for future reference.[1]

- Exercise on a regular basis. It's good for your mind, your body, and your mood.
- Relax your muscles. Stretch. Splurge on a nice hot stone massage. Take a long, hot, soothing bubble bath with an exotic blooming bath bomb that costs way too much. Catch some quality z's. Shamelessly invest in a sleep mask and proudly wear it.
- Practice focused and deep breathing.
- Eat responsibly from all the food groups.
- Take things down a notch. It's okay to disconnect from your technology for more than an hour at a time. It's okay to drive in the granny lane. It's okay to break big jobs down into little tasks and slowly get the bigger task done in those bite-sized pieces.
- Press pause. Do something to relax your mind, such as meditation, yoga, or prayer, or take a walk in the woods.
- Take up (or revisit) a hobby. Give yourself at least thirty minutes a day to enjoy doing something (not transition related) that gives you joy and takes your mind off things for a little while.

- Practice positive chit-chat. If you're feeling overwhelmed, talk about those overwhelming feelings with a trusted other or even internally with yourself.
- Try to laugh more and stop putting so much pressure on yourself. Realize that there is only so much in the universe you can actually control.
- Isolate the cause of your stress and figure out ways to reduce those feelings. For example, if you are stressed because you can't land a job interview, then have a good career counselor look over your resume. Maybe your resume sucks and someone who knows what she is doing might be able to easily fix it for you. *Just saying.*

Of course, if self-help techniques aren't working for you and the stress level is getting out of control, then consider getting help from a professional. Visit the family readiness center on the military installation nearest you and ask about arranging a confidential meeting with a military family life counselor (MFLC).

Understand How Everyone Really Feels about the Move

You may be physically relocating to a new city, state, or country. You may be moving from on base or on post to a new neighborhood off of it. You might be staying put right where you are. You might not have a clue about where you are going to move, or even if you are going to physically move at all.

Make no mistake about it, however: You are moving, even if it is only figuratively speaking. How do you feel about that, and how does your family (if you are blessed enough to have one) feel about it, too?

It is important in the beginning of transition process to talk about what is about to happen and the possibilities as they stand at the moment. Nobody likes to feel left out of such conversations, particularly when they have a direct impact. So don't leave anyone out.

Instead, communicate clearly with one another. Strive for a genuine understanding. It is equally important at this critical time to accept and respect those feelings even if you don't share them.

For example, you may want to retire and get a high-speed defense contracting job working inside the Beltway in DC. Your spouse may have no interest whatsoever in living in the city or anywhere near it. It is better to know there is dissent in the beginning of your transition than to assume it doesn't exist at all. It will save you ample heartache as you move along and decisions have to be made. After all, you can always work out the differences. Ignorance, however, is hopeless and can be incredibly damaging to your career and to your life.

Begin to Discuss Important Questions about the Future

What the world thinks you should do and what you want to do are sometimes at odds with one another. *Showtime, Sparky.* As you stand before this crossroads in your life, you have to figure out what is next for you. There won't be a set of orders coming down that specifies the details for you, and you are the final approving authority.

These are some of the types of important questions you may want to start thinking about now and begin discussing in greater detail:

- What do you want to do after leaving the military behind? Do you need to smoothly transition into a new job to keep the bills paid and continue your current standard of living? Is college in your immediate future instead? Or maybe a combination of the two is a possibility?
- Where do you fancy this new civilian life happening? Will you be sheltering in place or packing up everything you own and moving one more time, just for old time's sake? Who's going to pay for that, by the way?
- How are you going to finance this new civilianized lifestyle? What are your income streams? Do you have them? Do you need them?
- How will you continue financially planning for your ultimate retirement from the workforce?
- If you do need to find a job, what kind of job do you want and where would you ideally like this job to be located? Is there a market for it, and are you qualified, by civilian job market standards, for it? What is important to you in your next job? Does it have to pay well? What does that mean to you? Does it have to have advancement possibilities? Where do you see yourself ultimately being on some invisible org chart?
- How are you going to ensure continued health care, dental, and vision benefits for yourself and your family as you transition out? What about when the umbilical cord to Uncle Sam is cut, if indeed it will be severed? What then?
- After all the transition trauma has passed and the dust has settled, how do you see you and your family living the new version of your everyday life?

• What is important to you, your spouse, and your kids? Is it achievable, or will you have to cut corners in the short term to realize long-term gains?

There may be other questions to think about and discuss as well. The point is that you have to start somewhere.

Consider investing in a spiral notebook and a good pen. Start jotting down all the questions you can think of and keep them in one place. Expect to go back to that list and add to it along the way.

Clarity of vision doesn't have to be complicated. It doesn't even have to be clear in the beginning. It just has to be organized.

Expect an Initial Loss of Identity

In the military, you knew exactly who you were and what you were responsible for doing. You had a specific rank and a specific job. You knew the people who worked around you, for you, and above you. You were an instrumental component of a coherent team. You were expected to make big things happen throughout your military career, and you did that successfully.

Once you've made the decision to leave it all behind, you enter a no-man's-land of sorts. While you are in the process of transitioning, how others see you (and maybe even how you see yourself) may begin to change.

There Is a Traitor among Us . . . and You Are It

You are still in the military for the moment, but you are eventually leaving. *Willingly*, assuming this transition is one of your own choice. You are willingly leaving others behind who will continue on with the good fight without you by their side to support them, and that is okay. It is your turn to do so. Just don't expect everyone else to feel the same way you do. Where you feel excitement and anticipation, others may feel animosity, jealousy, and even low-key anger. It will help to have emotional and perhaps even tactical strategies in place for dealing with this type of blowback before you experience it firsthand.

Emotionally speaking, you do not need to waste your precious transition time worrying about the insecurities of others, even those you may care deeply about professionally. You have enough on your plate to deal with during this stressful time already.

On a tactical level, perhaps you can remind that person that his day to move on will eventually come, too. Regardless, keep yourself focused on what you need to do, while remaining proud of all that you have done already.

Forging a New Post-Uniform Identity

According to Gallup research, 55 percent of the people in the United States define themselves by their job instead of thinking of work as what they do for a living.[2] In the military, it may even be harder to separate your job from your identity because the two are often so dependent on one another.

Once you have transitioned out of uniform, however, you may have to establish yourself in a new workforce or, at the very least, in a new role within a familiar one.

Semper Gumby (Always Flexible)

One of the most important things you can do as you transition from one world to the next is be and remain flexible.

If you are vaguely familiar with Murphy's law, then you have a good understanding of the situation already. Everything may not always go as you planned. You may even experience disappointment along the way.

If you are truly open to and welcome the concept of flexibility, however, then the universe is more likely to play nice with you. You might even be surprised one day to discover that those so-called disappointments couldn't have worked out better for you if you had tried.

THE MILITARY MOTIONS YOU HAVE TO GO THROUGH TO GET OUT

You may be more than ready to take off your uniform, slip on some civilian clothes, and mosey out the door. The DoD, however, says, *Not so fast, buddy*. You have more than a few logistical loose ends to take care of before Uncle Sam gives you the coveted holy grail of all military documents, the DD 214, "Certificate of Release or Discharge from Active Duty."

Visit the TAP and Get Your Preseparation Counseling

Why don't we just call it what it is? The Transition Assistance Program (TAP) office is that happy place where all service members must go in order to

Military Life Cycle Model

By 2015, the Transition Assistance Program (TAP) Military Life Cycle (MLC) model will initiate a Service member's transition preparation at the onset of their military career (both Active Duty and Guard/Reserve). The model outlines key points in time or, "touch points," throughout a Service member's career to align their military career with their civilian career goals. It promotes awareness of the Career Readiness Standards (CRS) Service members must meet long before separating from Active Duty and enables transition to become a well-planned, organized progression of skill building and career readiness preparation.

KEY FEATURES

Standardized activities occur at key touch points throughout a Service member's career. The following list is an example of some of the activities that may occur during each phase that vary slightly for each Service.

1st Permanent Duty Station (Active); 1st Home Station/Initial Drilling Weekends (Reserve)
Develop IDP
Complete Financial Planning *(e.g., budget)*
Register at Department of Veterans Affairs (VA) eBenefits (www.ebenefits.va.gov)
Complete (aptitudes, interests, strengths, and/or skills) assessment

Re-enlistment
Update IDP
Adjust Financial Planning documentation *(e.g., budget)*
Review Military Occupational Code (MOC) alignment to civilian occupations

Promotion
Update IDP
Adjust Financial Planning documentation *(e.g., budget)*
Review MOC alignment

Change of Duty Station
Update IDP
Adjust Financial Planning documentation *(e.g., budget)*

Deployment and Redeployment / Mobilization and Demobilization / Deactivation
Complete all applicable CRS requirements
Adjust Financial Planning documentation *(e.g., budget)*
Confirm eBenefits registration

Major Life Events
Adjust Financial Planning documentation *(e.g., budget)*
Confirm eBenefits
Review/update (aptitudes, interests, strengths, and/or skills) assessment

Separation, Retirement, or Release from Active Duty
Complete pre-separation counseling to plan/prepare for transition
Develop an ITP (based on IDP) to determine how to achieve career goals
Attend required Transition GPS courses and complete all activities to meet CRS
Participate in Capstone to verify CRS completion

KEY FEATURES

>> Integrates transition preparation throughout a Service member's military career

>> Offers Service members education, training, and individualized attention at key touch points with standardized activities throughout their military career as part of their civilian career preparation

>> Initiates early Individual Development Plan (IDP) that becomes a Service member's individual Transition Plan (ITP); adaptable as changes occur in rank, military occupation, proficiencies, goals, and/or family circumstances

ADVANTAGES

>> **Service Members** – Provides the time and resources to plan for their inevitable transition from Active Duty

>> **Commanders** – Reduces mission impact as many transition-related actions are completed during the normal course of business instead of at the end of a Service member's time on Active Duty

>> **Military Departments** – Allows increased flexibility for transition service delivery

>> **Nation** – Service member planning and alignment with military-to-civilian labor market skills facilitates talent flow from the Military to the civilian sector and strengthens the recruiting pipeline for the future All-Volunteer Force

>> **Service Providers** – Promotes more predictable resource requirements as transition assistance is provided at pre-determined points

transition or retire out of the service. It is where you will receive a mandatory preseparation counseling briefing and attend transition-related workshops designed to prepare you for life after life in the military. It is where you check off all the blocks you need to check off in order to walk out the door, and it is also where you learn all about your potential benefits and entitlements.

Each branch of service has its own TAP (with some slight name variations), but the basic offerings available through each one are fairly consistent.

Service Branch Transition Assistance Programs (TAPs)

U.S. Army
Soldier for Life—Transition Assistance Program
https://www.sfl-tap.army.mil
[Program was formerly known as Army Career and Alumni Program (ACAP)]

U.S. Navy
Transition Assistance Program
https://www.cnic.navy.mil/ffr/family_readiness/fleet_and_family_support_program/transition_assistance.html

U.S. Air Force
Transition Assistance Program
http://www.afpc.af.mil/Transition-Assistance-Program

U.S. Marine Corps
Transition Readiness Program
http://www.usmc-mccs.org/index.cfm/services/career/transition-readiness/

U.S. Coast Guard
Office of Work-Life Programs, Transition Assistance Program
https://www.uscg.mil/worklife/transition_assistance.asp

If you are smart, you will take full advantage of every workshop, counseling session, and briefing offered through the TAP. It doesn't cost you anything, except your time and attention, and you will learn so much from it.

If you are married, plan to take your spouse with you, too. Two heads, as they say, are always better than one when facing a tough challenge ahead.

The DoD has greatly improved TAP over the last few years by carefully listening to service members and their families, veterans, service providers, and other stakeholders within the military communities and changing the way services are offered.

TAP is now TAP GPS, and it is defined as a lifecycle process that actually starts when the service member first enters active duty and continues throughout his or her military career. This paradigm shift is not insignificant.

A typical schedule of events and what each one involves follows.

Mandatory Preseparation Briefing

When you are between twelve and twenty-four months of getting out, but no later than ninety days before separation, the DoD wants you to begin the final TAP process by attending a mandatory preseparation counseling session.

During a preseparation counseling, you receive an overview of the programs and services available during your transition from a qualified TAP counselor.[3] You will be required to complete an Individual Transition Plan (ITP), a document that outlines the actions you need to take in order to achieve your transition goals, and a DD 2648 or DD 2648-1, "Preseparation Counseling Checklist." You generally have to complete this required training before you can do anything else within the TAP.

When exactly should you plan to attend preseparation counseling?

If you are planning to transition out of service, try to go at least one year prior to your separation from service. If you are retiring out of service, plan to go there at least two years before your retirement.

Five-Day TAP GPS or Executive TAP (for Senior Officers)

The five-day TAP Goals, Plans, Successes (GPS) is a week when "the focus of the curriculum is to connect the service member with professional helping agencies based on the need for support and guidance before they separate."[4]

It is not just a week off from work. If you are tempted to skip portions of it or seek a waiver from your boss to get out of it altogether, don't. Plan to attend every single minute of it.

By just showing up and listening, you will be doing yourself a huge favor. You will be gaining new information on many levels, and information is

SERVICE MEMBER PRE-SEPARATION/TRANSITION COUNSELING AND CAREER READINESS STANDARDS EFORM FOR SERVICE MEMBERS SEPARATING, RETIRING, RELEASED FROM ACTIVE DUTY (REFRAD)

SECTION I - PRIVACY ACT STATEMENT

AUTHORITY: 10 U.S.C. 1142, Preparation Counseling; transmittal of medical records to Department of Veterans Affairs.

PURPOSE(S): To record pre-separation counseling services and benefits requested by and provided to Service members; to identify pre-separation counseling areas of interest as a basis for development of an Individual Transition Plan (ITP). The signed pre-separation counseling checklist will be maintained in the Service member's official personnel file. Title 10 USC 1142, requires that not later than 90 days before the date of separation, for anticipated losses, pre-separation counseling for Service members be made available. For unanticipated losses, or in the event a member of a reserve component is being demobilized under circumstances in which operational requirements make the 90-day requirement unfeasible, pre-separation counseling shall be made available as soon as possible within the remaining period.

ROUTINE USE(S): Disclosure of records are generally permitted under 5 U.S.C. 552a(b) of the Privacy Act of 1974, as amended. Applicable Blanket Routine Use(s) are: Law Enforcement Routine Use, Congressional Inquiries, Disclosure to the Department of Justice for Litigation Routine Use, Disclosure of Information to the National Archives and Records Administration Routine Use, and Data Breach Remediation Purposes Routine Use.

To the Department of Veterans Affairs for the purpose of available benefits to the Service member.
The complete list of DoD Blanket Routine Uses can be found online at http://dpcld.defense.gov/Privacy/SORNsindex/BlanketRoutineUses.aspx
The applicable system of records notice is: DMDC 01, Defense Manpower Data Center Data Base
The SORNs may be found at http://dpcld.defense.gov/Privacy/SORNsindex/DOD-wide-SORN-Article-View/Article/570563/dmdc-01/

DISCLOSURE: Disclosure is voluntary however it may not be possible to initiate preseparation counseling and other transition assistance services or develop an Individual Transition Plan (ITP) for a Service member if the information is not provided.

SECTION II – SERVICE MEMBER PERSONAL INFORMATION

1. NAME		2. DOD ID NUMBER	3. GRADE	4. DATE OF BIRTH	5. SERVICE	5a. COMPONENT
6. UNIT NAME		6a. UNIT ID CODE		6b. MILITARY INSTALLATION		
7. ANTICIPATED DATE OF SEPARATION	7a. REASON FOR SEPARATION		7b. TYPE OF SEPARATION		8. DATE FORM WAS INITIATED	

9. MEMBER ALLOWS THIS FORM TO BE SENT TO FEDERAL AGENCIES FOR ADDITIONAL TRANSITION ASSISTANCE POST SEPARATION:

9a. MEMBER ALLOWS THIS FORM TO BE SENT TO FEDERAL AND OTHER AGENCIES WHO LOOK FOR CRITICAL LANGUAGE SKILLS AND/OR REGIONAL EXPERTISE THAT COULD BE VITAL DURING TIMES OF NEED, CRISIS, AND/OR NATIONAL EMERGENCIES:

9b. POST-SEPARATION EMAIL:	9c. POST-SEPARATION PHONE NUMBER:

10. MILITARY MEMBER/CAREGIVER/LEGAL GUARDIAN/DESIGNEE GOING TO BE PRESENT DURING PRE-SEPARATION COUNSELING:

SECTION III – PRE-SEPARATION / TRANSITION COUNSELING, PRE-SEPARATION / TRANSITION COUNSELING NEEDS ASSESSMENT, REVIEW, AND VERIFICATION TO MEET CAREER READINESS STANDARDS (CRS), AND VOW COMPLIANCE

Service members shall be counseled on all items prescribed in Title 10, United States Code (U.S.C.), Chapter 58, Sections 1142(b) (1-17), Sections 1143, 1143a, 1144, 1145, 1146, 1147, 1148, 1149, 1150, 1151, and 1154, and DoD policies; involuntarily separated Service members have alternative benefits and programs that apply to them. Service member completed the following to meet Career Readiness Standards (CRS):

*Required

	Pre-Sep Assessment	Capstone CRS Review
11. Completed Pre-Separation Counseling: *		
12. Completed the Veteran Affairs (VA) Benefits Briefings I and II: *		
13. Completed the Department of Labor (DOL) Employment Workshop: *		
14. Registered on eBenefits *		
15. Prepared a criterion-based Financial Plan for military to civilian transition *		
16. Completed a criterion-based Individual Transition Plan (ITP) *		
17. Completed a Continuum of Military Service Opportunity Counseling (Required Active Component Only)		
18. Evaluated transferability of military skills to civilian workforce / Complete DoD Standardized Gap Analysis *		
19. Documented requirements and eligibility for licensure, certification, and apprenticeship *		
20. Completed an assessment tool to identify personal interests and leanings regarding career selection *		
21. Completed a job application package or received a job offer letter *		
22. Received a DOL Gold Card and understands post- 9/11 Veterans have priority at DOL American Job Centers *		
23. Completed an assessment tool to identify aptitudes, interests, strengths, or skills		
24. Completed a comparison of higher academic or technical training institution options		
25. Completed a college, university, or career technical training application or received an acceptance letter		
26. Confirmed one-on-one counseling with a higher education or career technical training institution advisor		

27. I WAS COUNSELED AND RECEIVED DOCUMENTATION ON ALL ITEMS IN SECTION III, WHICH INCLUDES ALL ITEMS LISTED ON THE PRE-SEPARATION / TRANSITION COUNSELING ADDENDUM SHEET:

28. PRE-SEPARATION / TRANSITION COUNSELING WAS COMPLETED WITH 89 DAYS OR LESS REMAINING BEFORE SEPARATION:

28a. PRE-SEPARATION / TRANSITION COUNSELING COMPLETED 89 DAYS OR LESS JUSTIFICATION:

29. SERVICE MEMBER SIGNATURE & DATE	30. TRANSITION COUNSELOR SIGNATURE & DATE

DD FORM 2648, NOV2016   PREVIOUS EDITION IS OBSOLETE.   Page 1 of 3

SECTION IV – OTHER REQUIREMENTS

31. EVALUATED POST-TRANSITION TRANSPORTATION REQUIREMENTS AND DEVELOPED A PLAN TO MEET PERSONAL/FAMILY NEEDS:

32. EVALUATED POST-TRANSITION HOUSING REQUIREMENTS AND DEVELOPED A PLAN TO MEET PERSONAL/FAMILY NEEDS:

SECTION V – OTHER CURRICULUM ATTENDANCE

33. ACCESSING HIGHER EDUCATION TRACK:

34. ENTREPRENEURSHIP TRACK:

34a. ADDITIONAL ENTREPRENEURSHIP TRACK TRAINING (8 WEEK COURSE):

35. CAREER TECHNICAL TRAINING TRACK:

SECTION VI – CAPSTONE REVIEW

36. SERVICE MEMBER SIGNATURE & DATE	37. TRANSITION COUNSELOR SIGNATURE & DATE

SECTION VII – COMMANDER OR COMMANDER'S DESIGNEE VERIFICATION

38. APPLICABLE CAREER READINESS STANDARDS MET:	41. COMMANDER OR COMMANDER'S DESIGNEE SIGNATURE & DATE
39. VIABLE ITP COMPLETED:	
40. WARM HANDOVERS EXECUTED:	

SECTION VIII – WARM HANDOVER TO SUPPORTING AGENCIES CONTACT INFORMATION

42. VETERANS AFFAIRS:

43. DEPARTMENT OF LABOR:

44. OTHER RESOURCE:

SECTION IX – REMARKS

45. REMARKS:

45. REMARKS (CONT.):

power. Not only will you and your family learn how to best navigate this impending transition, but you will also have the opportunity to bond with other service members and spouses who are essentially going through the same process. Never underestimate the power of an expanded network.

Specific workshops you may be able to take advantage of, depending on your location and the services offered there, include:

- *Department of Labor (DoL) Employment Workshop*: In this workshop you will learn how to conduct an effective job search campaign. You will also discover how to apply for unemployment benefits though the DoL while learning about potential state benefits available to you as a veteran.
- *Veterans Affairs (VA) Briefings I and II*: After you complete these briefings, you should know how exactly to apply for those veterans health, education, home loan guaranty, insurance, and disability benefits for which you are eligible. You will also know how to connect with VA staff for further assistance should you require it.
- *MOC Crosswalk*: You know what you did in the military, but what can you do with those skills outside of it? In the Military Occupational Code (MOC) Crosswalk portion of the GPS course, you will learn how to find out.
- *Financial Planning for Transition Workshop*: This is a great addition to the TAP. This is when you find out whether you can really afford to get out. It should be training that you do long before this moment in time, but at least it is available at this point. In this workshop, you will create a twelve-month postseparation budget. Enlightening stuff.
- *Individual Transition Plan (ITP) Review*: If you want to get out of the military, the military says you have to have a plan, or, more specifically, an Individual Transition Plan (ITP). You may have started this in your preseparation counseling. You will continue to review it here.

Two-Day Optional Tracks

- *Entrepreneurship Track: Boots to Business*: If you've ever dreamed of being your own boss, then definitely take this track. The Small Business Administration (SBA) hosts it, and you will learn about the benefits and challenges of entrepreneurship and the steps required for business ownership through the SBA's "Boots to Business." After successfully completing this track, you will be given the opportunity to enroll in an optional eight-week online entrepreneurship course. In that course, you will complete a business plan and be connected with a successful business mentor to assist you with the start-up process.

- *Career Technical Training Track*: You might be ready to do something different from what you did in service, or you might seek more advanced technical training in what you have done. The instructors in this track will help to explore options and even apply to a technical school. You will have the opportunity to meet with career technical training experts and/or VA educational vocational counselors.

- *Accessing Higher Education Track*: Not everyone wants to go straight from serving in uniform to working a nine-to-five job. Some of you want to go to college, taking advantage of those generous VA educational benefits. In this workshop, you'll learn how to select and apply to a good school. You will learn what it takes to be a good student (if you do not already know), and you will even have the opportunity to schedule some one-on-one time with an education counselor or with a college representative.

Capstone

Once you have made it to Capstone, you are in the home stretch. This is another mandatory piece of your transition process that happens when you have theoretically finished all the coursework and briefings that TAP has to offer.

During Capstone, you meet with your commander or someone appointed by him or her to verify that you have met the Career Readiness Standards (CRS) and you have a workable Individual Transition Plan.

The concept is simple: If you decide to leave the military behind, the DoD at least wants to make sure you have your transition act together. They also want to avoid having to pay big bucks down the road because of veteran unemployment claims. It ends up being a win-win for everyone.

DoD TAP Career Readiness Standards

1. Complete the Individual Transition Plan (ITP) documenting your personal employment, higher education, career technical training, and/or entrepreneurship goals, actions, and milestones.

2. Complete an integrated twelve-month post-separation budget.
3. Register on the VA eBenefits site.
4. Complete Continuum of Military Service Opportunity Counseling (Active Component to Reserve Component only).
5. Evaluate transferability of military skills to the civilian workforce and complete the gap analysis provided during the MOC Crosswalk.
6. Identify requirements and eligibility for certification, licensure, and apprenticeship in the service member's desired potential career field.
7. Complete a standardized individual assessment tool to identify personal interests and leanings that will enable informed decision-making regarding career selection.
8. Receive Department of Labor (DOL) Gold Card for American Job Centers. The Gold Card provides six months of priority services for post-9/11 veterans at any DOL American Job Center, including DOL-funded employment and training programs, case management, skills assessment and interest surveys, career guidance, and job search assistance.
9. Complete job application package or receive job offer letter. The package must include a private or public sector resume, personal and professional references, and at least two submitted job applications.

If you are seeking higher education or career technical training, you must:

1. Complete an assessment tool to identify aptitudes, interests, strengths, and skills used to inform your decision about selecting higher education and career technical training toward a desired future career field.
2. Complete a comparison of academic or training institution choices.
3. Complete a college, university, or technical training application or receive an acceptance letter.
4. Confirm your one-on-one counseling with a college, university, or technical training institution advisor or counselor.

Source: https://www.dodtap.mil/career_readiness_standards.html

Is TAP Vital to Your Transition Success?

You have to do pieces of TAP whether you want to or not. If you are smart, you will take advantage of the entire program.

If you are a believer in surveys, TAP GPS works. According to the 2016 Blue Star Families Military Family Lifestyle Survey, 56 percent of veterans who attended Transition GPS reported that it prepared them for a successful transition.[5] Forty-nine percent of veterans who reported attending any transition programming said that it also helped to prepare them for a successful transition.[6]

Of course, your ultimate personal and professional success because of the new and improved TAP GPS assumes that individual leaders will wholeheartedly support it. While that *always* happens in theory, it does not always happen in practice.

UNDERSTANDING YOUR POTENTIAL POST-UNIFORM BENEFITS

In VA Briefings I and II, as noted above, you will learn the finer details about your benefits and entitlements. After you have completed those briefings, you should know how exactly to apply for your own VA health, education, home loan guaranty, insurance, and disability benefits if you are eligible. You will also learn how to connect with VA staff for further assistance should you require it.

Those are important briefings for you to go to, but they also are not the only place where you can learn about them. The VA benefits website details it all, too.

One of the key things you should note, in relationship to VA benefits, is that some of them are time sensitive, meaning you have a certain time period in which to apply for them. Outside of that specified time period, you are out of luck.

Below you find brief explanations regarding some of the most popular VA benefits. For the most up-to-date information about all of your potential benefits, however, visit the VA website online at http://www.benefits.va.gov/benefits/.

The Department of Veterans Affairs (VA)

As you transition from someone who wears a uniform into someone who used to, you may come to rely a great deal on the VA for a number of potential benefits in your life.

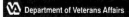 **Department of Veterans Affairs**

VETERANS BENEFITS TIMETABLE
Information for Veterans Recently Separated from Active Military Service

BENEFITS AND SERVICES		TIME LIMIT	WHERE TO APPLY
Disability Compensation: VA pays monthly compensation to veterans for disabilities incurred or aggravated during military service. This benefit is not subject to Federal or State income tax. Entitlement is established from the date of separation if the claim is filed within one year from separation. Generally, military retirement pay is reduced by any VA compensation received. Income from Special Separation Benefits (SSB) and Voluntary Separation Incentives (VSI) affects the amount of VA compensation paid.		None	Any VA office or call 1-800-827-1000 or file at www.va.gov
Veterans Pension: Pension is a needs-based benefit paid to wartime veterans, who meet certain age or non-service connected disability requirements.		None	
Medical: VA provides a wide range of health care services to veterans including treatment for military sexual trauma, and for conditions possibly related to exposure to Agent Orange, ionizing radiation, and other environmental hazards in the Persian Gulf. Generally, veterans must be enrolled in VA's Health Care System to receive care.		None	Any VA medical facility or call 1-877-222-8387 or file at www.va.gov
Combat Veterans: VA provides free health care for veterans who served in a theater of combat operations after November 11, 1998, for any illness possibly related to their service in that theater.	If discharged from active duty on or after January 28, 2003	Five years from date of discharge from active duty	
	If discharged from active duty before January 28, 2003, and were not enrolled as of January 28, 2008	Until January 27, 2011	
Dental: Veterans may receive one-time dental treatment if they were not provided treatment within 90 days before separation from active duty. The time limit does not apply to veterans with dental conditions resulting from service-connected wounds or injuries.		180 days from separation	
Education and Training: Up to 36 months of benefits for:	Montgomery GI Bill - Active Duty (Chapter 30)	10 years from release from last period of active duty. Limited extensions available.	Any VA office or call 1-888-GIBILL-1 (1-888-442-4551) or file at www.gibill.va.gov
	OR Post-9/11 GI Bill (Chapter 33)	15 years form last discharge or separation. Limited extensions available.	
	OR Montgomery GI Bill - Selected Reserve (Chapter 1606)	Eligibility expires on the date the individual is separated from the Selected Reserves.	
	OR Reserve Educational Assistance Program (REAP/Chapter 1607)	No time limit as long as individual remains in the same level of the Ready Reserve from which called to active duty. REAP participants who separated from the Selected Reserve after completing their service contract under other than dishonorable conditions are eligible for REAP benefits for 10 years after they are separated from the Selected Reserve.	
Vocational Rehabilitation and Employment: VA helps veterans with service-connected disabilities prepare for, find and keep suitable employment. For veterans with serious service-connected disabilities, VA also offers services to improve their ability to live as independently as possible. Some of the services offered are: job search, vocational evaluation, career exploration, vocational training, education training and rehabilitation service.		Generally 12 years from VA notice to veteran of at least a 10 percent disability rating.	Any VA office or call 1-800-827-1000 or file at www.va.gov
Home Loan: Veterans with qualifying service are eligible for VA home loan benefits including guaranteed loans for the purchase of a home, or to build, repair, and improve homes. Certain disabled veterans can receive grants to have their homes specially adapted to their needs. Native Americans living on Trust Land may qualify for a direct home loan.		None	Any VA office or call 1-888-768-2132 or visit www.ebenefits.va.gov

VETERANS BENEFITS TIMETABLE (Continued)

BENEFITS AND SERVICES		TIME LIMIT	WHERE TO APPLY
Life Insurance:	**SGLI (Servicemembers' Group Life Insurance)** is low-cost life insurance for active duty Servicemembers and reservists. It is available in $50,000 increments up to a maximum of $400,000. SGLI coverage begins automatically when the servicemember enters service or changes duty status.	Coverage continues for 120 days from date of separation, or up to two years if totally disabled at the time of separation from service.	http://www. benefits. va.gov/insurance or call 1-800-419-1473
	Traumatic Injury Protection under Servicemembers' Group Life Insurance (TSGLI) is a traumatic injury protection rider under Servicemembers' Group Life Insurance (SGLI) that provides for payment to any member of the uniformed services covered by SGLI who sustains a traumatic injury that results in certain severe losses. TSGLI is retroactive for members who sustain a qualifying loss as a direct result of injuries incurred on or after October 7, 2001, through November 30, 2005, regardless of whether they had SGLI coverage. TSGLI pays a benefit of between $25,000 and $100,000 depending on the loss incurred. In order for a veteran to qualify for a TSGLI payment, they must have incurred a qualifying loss as a result of a traumatic event that occurred while they were in the service (the loss itself can occur after separation.) The injury does NOT have to be combat or service related.	Coverage continues through midnight of the date of discharge. There is no time limit to apply for a TSGLI payment. However, the member/ veteran must suffer the loss within 2 years of their injury to qualify for payment.	
	VGLI (Veterans' Group Life Insurance) is lifetime renewable term life insurance for veterans. It is available in increments of $10,000 up to $400,000. Initial VGLI coverage cannot exceed the amount of SGLI coverage in force at the time of the servicemember's separation from service but additional coverage of $25,000 can be requested on each five-year anniversary up to the maximum coverage available. Premiums are age-based.	Must apply within 240 days of separation, or 1 year and 120 days if proof of good health is provided. Those on the 2-year disability extension are automatically converted to VGLI at the end of the 2-year period.	
	FSGLI (Family Servicemembers' Group Life Insurance) is life insurance that provides automatic coverage to the spouse and dependent children of servicemembers insured under SGLI. Spousal coverage is available up to a maximum of $100,000, but may not exceed the servicemember's coverage amount. Premiums for spousal coverage are age based. Dependent children are automatically covered for $10,000 for which there is no cost. Child coverage is automatic with SGLI coverage regardless of whether the member has spouse coverage.	Coverage terminates 120 days after servicemember is released from service. Spouse may convert to a commercial policy.	
	S-DVI (Service-Disabled Veterans' Insurance) also called "RH" insurance, is life insurance for service-connected disabled veterans. The basic coverage is $10,000. A $20,000 supplemental policy is available if premium payments for the basic policy are waived due to total disability.	For basic, must apply within two years from date of notification of service-connected disability. For supplemental, must apply within one year of approval of waiver of premiums.	http://www. benefits.va.gov/ insurance or call 1-800-669-8477
	VMLI (Veterans' Mortgage Life Insurance) is mortgage protection insurance available to those severely disabled veterans who have received grants for Specially-Adapted Housing from VA. Maximum coverage of $200,000.	Must apply before age 70.	
Reemployment: The Department of Labor's web site www.dol.gov contains information on employment and reemployment rights of members of the uniformed services.		For military service over 180 days, must apply for reemployment with employer within 90 days from separation. Shorter periods to apply if service is less than 180 days.	Former employer
Unemployment Compensation: The unemployment compensation for ex-servicemenbers program is administered by the States as agents of the Federal government. The Department of Labor's web site www.dol.gov contains links for each State's benefits, including the District of Columbia and Puerto Rico.		Limited time	State Employment Office (bring your DD-214)

FOR ADDITIONAL INFORMATION VISIT THE VA WEB SITE AT WWW.VA.GOV

PROTECT YOUR INDENTITY

Your DD-214, *Certificate of Release or Discharge from Active Duty*, contains personal information. Keep it in a safe place. Protect yourself from identity theft. If you decide to file your DD-214 at a public records facility such as a court house or vital statistics agency, you may want to inquire about the level of security in place to limit public access to your document.

Disability Compensation

VA disability compensation is "a tax-free benefit paid to veterans with disabilities that are the result of a disease or injury incurred or aggravated during active military service."[7] Compensation may also be paid for disabilities that occur after life in service if they are considered related or secondary to disabilities that occurred while a veteran was in service.

Compensation is payable to any veteran with a service-connected disability rating of 10 percent or more who left the service under conditions other than dishonorable.

As you transition out of service, file a VA claim for disability. You can file it at any time, but it is smarter to do it now when you can more easily point to probable causes of potential problems. If you wait to file a VA claim later, it will be more difficult to prove that your disability is related to your time in the service.

Even if you don't think there is anything disabled about you or if you feel awkward doing it, file it anyway. There are many good reasons for doing so, even if it is not the first and foremost item on your little transition-laden mind.

- Disability pay is not subject to state or federal taxes.
- If you are rated disabled at 50 percent or higher and you are also retired from service, you get to keep the full amounts of disability and retirement pay. (If you are classified less than 50 percent disabled and you are also retired from service, then you can choose to offset your retirement pay with the VA compensation, making a portion of your military retirement tax-free.)
- Some states exempt disabled veterans from having to pay various taxes such as property taxes.
- Your children might be eligible for free in-state college tuition as a result of your disabled status.
- The VA provides medical care for disabled veterans.
- Veterans who are classified as disabled get federal employment hiring preferences.
- The minor knee pain you occasionally experience as a result of jumping out of planes could get much worse later on as you age.
- If you are 70 percent disabled, then the VA is obligated to pay nursing home expenses. That may not be high on your list of priorities now, but you might feel differently thirty or forty years from now.

DISABILITY COMPENSATION

SEPARATION HEALTH ASSESSMENT FOR SERVICEMEMBERS

OVERVIEW

The separation health assessment was developed to provide a single separation examination that supports the Department of Veterans Affairs (VA) disability compensation program and the Department of Defense (DoD) mandatory separation history and physical examination. The assessment captures current health information in a way that is accessible by DoD and VA.

WHO CONDUCTS THE EXAM?

- VA will conduct the exam for Servicemembers who file a complete application for disability compensation while having at least 90 days remaining on active duty.

- DoD will conduct the exam for Servicemembers who do not file a claim for disability compensation, or who file a claim with less than 90 days remaining on active duty.

ASSESSMENT BENEFITS

- Provides a comprehensive medical evaluation at separation, which

  ○ Documents current and past medical concerns identified during military career, and

  ○ Assesses current health status and medical history.

- DoD can use assessment results to identify and evaluate illnesses and injuries that are potentially caused by occupational exposures and physical hazards in military workplaces. This may result in eliminating these exposures and hazards and preventing future illnesses and injuries.

- Assessments are an efficient way for VA to identify service-connected conditions.

- Assessments allow more accurate prediction of future healthcare needs.

- Information gathered from the assessment can be used focus Veteran outreach efforts.

★ ★ ★ ★

U.S. Department of Veterans Affairs

ACTIONS

Servicemembers filing a claim for VA disability compensation should:

- Submit an application for VA benefits (VA Form 21-526EZ, Application for Disability Compensation and Related Compensation Benefits) between 90 and 180 days prior to separation or retirement,

- Submit a copy of service treatment records (STRs) from the current period of service,

- Complete, sign, and submit DD Form 2807-1, "Report of Medical History, and

- VA will schedule an exam to evaluate claimed conditions.

Servicemembers in the following categories must complete and sign DD Form 2807-1, Report of Medical History, and DoD will complete the separation exam in coordination with the appropriate out-processing center for:

- Servicemembers are not filing a claim for VA disability

- Servicemembers with less than 90 days prior to discharge or retirement

Note: Servicemembers with less than 90 days until discharge may still file a pre-discharge claim for VA disability benefits; however, the Servicemember must ensure the separation examination is completed by DoD.

FREQUENTLY ASKED QUESTIONS (FAQS)

Question: I am not filing a VA disability claim, why do I have to get an exam?

Answer: The assessment can uncover medical conditions that occurred during military service for which you may be unaware. If you choose to file a VA disability claim later, the information contained in the assessment may be essential in establishing that a disability was incurred in or aggravated by your military service. The assessment also provides information that can be used to identify and prevent illnesses and injuries caused by military service. Assessment information can also be used to more accurately predict healthcare services required for Veterans.

Question: What does an assessment include?

Answer:

- Subjective Assessment of Health: You will complete the DD Form 2807-1, "Report of Medical History" prior to your scheduled exam. The VA or DoD examiner performing the exam will review the answers and ensure claimed contentions are addressed in the examiner's section of the form or in the exam report, which becomes part of the record.

- Objective Assessment of Health: The examiner will review your complete medical history(including the DD Form 2807-1) and your current health status to determine if there is a need for further treatment or evaluations regarding any medical concerns.

Question: Can I submit a VA disability claim while still on active duty?

Answer: Yes, VA accepts disability claims from separating Servicemembers through two Pre-Discharge programs:

- o Benefits Delivery at Discharge (BDD) Program allows a Servicemember to submit a claim for disability compensation 60 to 180 days prior to separation, retirement, or release from active duty or demobilization
- o Quick Start Program allows a Servicemember to submit a claim for disability compensation 1 to 59 days prior to separation, retirement, or release from active duty or demobilization

For more information about filing a pre-discharge claim, please refer to the Pre-Discharge Programs brochure. VA representatives are available at many military installations to assist with submitting VA disability claims through the Pre-Discharge Programs. A list of military installations with a VA representative can be found in the VA Facility Locator.

Question: How do I file a VA disability claim?

Answer: You can file a VA disability claim through eBenefits. You can also file a VA claim in person with a Veterans Service Organization (VSO) or a VA representative at a military installation. Submit a copy of your STRs from your current period of military service and any copies of private treatment records not associated with TRICARE referrals. You should receive information regarding eligibility and application requirements during your Transition Assistance Program (TAP) briefing.

For more information on VA disability benefits, call toll-free 1-800-827-1000 or visit VA's website. Instructions and claim forms may also be found on TRICARE online.

According to the VA, the best way to apply for disability compensation is to open an eBenefits (www.ebenefits.va.gov) account and apply for benefits online. You'll save yourself some paperwork angst by having the following on hand to assist you in the process:

- Your DD 214 (or equivalent)
- Doctor and hospital reports (i.e., medical evidence)
- Marriage certificate and children's birth certificates

If you do not want to apply through eBenefits, you can always complete and snail mail the VA Form 21-526EZ, "Application for Disability Compensation and Related Compensation Benefits."

The VA claims process is not exactly known for its lightning speed. You could receive benefits sooner, however, if you apply for them before you even get out of service through the Benefits Delivery at Discharge (BDD) or Quick Start pre-discharge programs.

MAKING THE PROCESS EASIER ON EVERYONE

You do not have to look too far in your world to find someone who has had less-than-stellar experiences with the VA claims process. While each case is different, there are some simple things you can do as you start the application process that may eliminate frustration along the way.

Read the instructions carefully on any forms you fill out. Understand what the form is asking for and provide the right information in the level of detail warranted. Do not leave any blanks. If something does not apply to you, enter NA for "not applicable." If you do not know the answer to a question, enter "Unknown."

Stick to providing the relevant facts and only the relevant facts on your application. When you add extraneous information, you confuse your claim and potentially prolong the processing time.

When you receive correspondence from the VA, read it carefully for content and context. Note any deadlines and do not miss them. Keep the paperwork you send and receive organized.

Consider creating a logbook that details your timeline of any VA-related activities as you begin this process. For example:

Date/Description
1 July 2018: Created account on eBenefits and applied for benefits.
15 August 2018: Spoke with John Smith (tele: xxx-xxx-xxxx) regarding status of claim and was told I should hear in writing by 30
Sept 18.

This may prove helpful to you as time goes by and should matters get more complicated.

In the process of working with the VA, you will most likely have to schedule doctor appointments. Do not miss them when you do.

Be patient. Strike that. Be an expert at being patient. Unless you have been living under a rock, you know the VA has not enjoyed the most flattering of headlines in recent years. While you may not be able to control the seemingly chaotic processes from the bureaucracy's side of the table, you can do your best to work with what you have.

Finally, consider getting help with the process from a veteran service officer (VSO). VSOs help you write and submit your benefits claim to the VA. Their services are free, and they will even assist with research, tracking, and appeals filing.[8] Visit http://nvf.org/veteran-service-officers/ for links to VSOs in your area.

Education and Training

The VA offers many benefits to help make you (and your family members) smart and marketable without going into major debt.

- The Post-9/11 GI Bill offers higher education and training benefits to veterans, service members, and their families who served after September 10, 2001. (Do not forget about the potential to transfer used benefits to your spouse or your children while it lasts, either.)
- The Montgomery GI Bill assists active duty and reservists with the pursuit of higher education degrees, certificates, and other education and training.

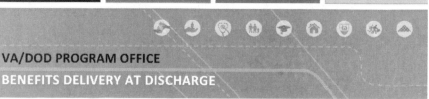
BENEFITS DELIVERY AT DISCHARGE (BDD)

If you are separating from active duty within the next 60 to 180 days, BDD can help you receive VA disability benefits sooner.

WHAT IS BENEFITS DELIVERY AT DISCHARGE?

The Benefits Delivery at Discharge (BDD) Program allows a servicemember to apply for disability compensation benefits from the Department of Veterans Affairs (VA) prior to retirement or separation from military service.

HOW CAN BDD HELP ME?

BDD is offered to accelerate receipt of VA disability benefits, with a goal of providing benefits within 60 days after release or discharge from active duty. BDD allows a servicemember with at least 60 days, but not more than 180 days, remaining on active duty to file a VA disability claim *prior to* separation. BDD requires a minimum of 60 days to allow sufficient time to complete the medical examination process (which may involve multiple specialty clinics) prior to separation from service.

HOW DO I GET STARTED?

Submit VA Form 21-526, or VA Form 21-526e, *Veteran's Application for Compensation and/or Pension*, and submit it to the nearest VA Regional Office. You can also complete your application on-line using Veterans Online Application (VONAPP). For the VA Regional Office nearest you, call the VA toll free number at 1-800-827-1000. Submit your service treatment records. Either your original records or copies are acceptable. Attend and complete all phases of your VA/DoD medical separation examination process.

WHAT ELSE SHOULD I KNOW?

BDD is a time-sensitive process. To receive your VA disability benefits within the goal of 60 days following separation, you must submit your claim 60 to 180 days prior to your release or retirement from active duty. This time is needed to complete your medical examinations before you leave your point of separation. If you are closer than 60 days to separation from service, you can submit a Quick Start claim.

U.S. Department
of Veterans Affairs

HOW CAN I GET MORE INFORMATION?

If you are on a military installation, contact your local Transition Assistance Office or ACAP Center (Army only) to schedule appointments to attend VA benefits briefings and learn how to initiate your claim. You can also call the VA toll-free number, 1-800-827-1000. Be sure to visit Military One Source for 24/7 access to helpful pre-separation and transition guides; employment, education, and relocation information, benefits checklist; and more.

For More Information Visit Our BDD website.

There are other VA education and training programs, too, such as:

- Reserve Educational Assistance Program
- Veterans Educational Assistance Program
- Survivors and Dependents Educational Assistance Program
- National Testing Program
- National Call to Service Program

To learn more about them, visit your education center or go online at http://www.benefits.va.gov/gibill/education_programs.asp.

Vocational Rehabilitation and Employment

If you are a veteran with a service-connected disability, then the VA will help you find and maintain gainful employment. They can help you with a job search, career exploration, and vocational training among other services.

If you have a serious service-connected disability, they can also provide you with services to help you live as independently as possible. Service members who have at least a 10 percent VA disability rating can generally use vocational rehabilitation services for a twelve-year period.

You can apply for vocational rehabilitation and employment benefits or for education or career counseling online through the eBenefits website (www.ebenefits.va.gov).

Home Loans

The VA provides a home loan guaranty benefit and other housing-related programs to help you buy, build, repair, retain, or adapt a home for your own personal use. VA home loans are provided by private lenders, such as banks and mortgage companies. VA guarantees a portion of the loan, enabling the lender to provide you with more favorable terms.

Life Insurance

As an active-duty service member, you understand the importance of planning for a worst-case scenario. While serving, you may have had adequate life insurance. When you retire or transition, the VA insurance you may have carried (SGLI, FSGLI, or TSGLI) eventually goes away, and you have to replace it with something else. Fortunately, you do have a little time between when you get out and when the coverage ends.

HOME LOAN GUARANTY

VA GUARANTEED LOAN

WHAT IS A VA GUARANTEED LOAN?

A VA-guaranteed loan can be used to:

- buy a home, either existing or pre-construction, as a primary residence
- refinance an existing loan

BENEFITS OF A VA GUARANTEED LOAN:

- Equal opportunity for all qualified Veterans to obtain a VA loan
- Reusable
- No down payment (unless required by the lender or the purchase price is more than the reasonable value of the property)
- No mortgage insurance
- One time VA funding fee that can be included in the loan 1
- Veterans receiving VA disability compensation are exempt from the VA funding fee
- VA limits certain closing costs a Veteran can pay
- Can be assumed by qualified persons
- Minimum property requirements to ensure the property is safe, sanitary, and sound
- VA staff dedicated to assisting Veterans who become delinquent on their loan

WHO IS ELIGIBLE?

Generally, the following people are eligible:

- Veterans who meet length of service requirements
- Servicemembers on active duty who have served a minimum period
- Certain Reservists and National Guard members
- Certain surviving spouses of deceased Veterans

Disabilities determined by VA to be related to your military service can lead to monthly non-taxable compensation, enrollment in the VA health care system, a 10-point hiring preference for federal employment and other important benefits. Ask your VA representative or Veterans Service Organization representative about Disability Compensation, Pension, Health Care, Caregiver Program, Career Services, Educational Assistance, Home Loan Guaranty, Insurance and/or Dependents and Survivors' Benefits.

★ ★ ★ ☆

U.S. Department
of Veterans Affairs

Note: There are other groups of individuals who may be eligible. To determine your eligibility, check eBenefits or contact VA Eligibility Center at 1-888-768-2132.

KEY UNDERWRITING CRITERIA:

- No maximum debt ratio; however lender must provide compensating factors if total debt ratio over 41%.

- No maximum loan amount; however, VA does limit its guaranty; Veterans can borrow up to $417,000 without a down payment in most of the country. Find out the limit in any county.

- Published residual income guidelines to ensure Veterans have the capacity to repay their obligations while accounting for all living expenses.

- No minimum credit score requirement, instead VA requires a lender to review the entire loan profile to make a lending decision.

- See the complete VA credit guidelines.

HOW DO I START THE PROCESS?

VA provides policy, guidelines and oversight of the program. Lenders provide financing for eligible Veterans. The guaranty allows Veterans to obtain a competitive loan without a down payment. Lenders need a Certificate of Eligibility (COE) to prove your entitlement. Most Veterans can obtain the COE online through eBenefits. Lenders also have the ability to request the COE on your behalf.

VA encourages prospective buyers to talk to several lenders to find one that fits their needs, knows the VA loan program, and offers competitive rates and terms.

Note: The VA appraisal is not intended to be an "inspection" of the property.

A Veteran should get expert advice from a qualified residential inspection service before legally committing to a purchase agreement. Veterans are also encouraged to have radon testing performed.

CAN VA HELP IF I'M HAVING TROUBLE MAKING PAYMENTS ON MY EXISTING LOAN?

VA Loan Technicians are trained to help Veteran borrowers retain their homes and avoid foreclosure. Please call toll-free 1-877-827-3702 to speak to a VA Loan Technician.

For more information visit our Home Loans website.

If you have coverage under the Servicemembers' Group Life Insurance (SGLI), then you will continue to have it for at least 120 days from the date of your separation or up to two years if you are totally disabled at the time of separation from service.

If you have Family Servicemembers' Group Life Insurance (FSGLI), then your coverage terminates 120 days after you (the service member) are released from service. Your spouse may convert it to a commercial policy, however.

If you have Traumatic Injury Protection under SGLI (TSGLI), then coverage continues through midnight of your date of discharge. Remember, there is no time limit to apply for a TSGLI payment, but the member/veteran must suffer the loss within two years of his injury to qualify for payment.

The VA offers options for you as a veteran, too.

Veterans Group Life Insurance (VGLI) is a lifetime renewable term insurance policy that you can get in increments of $10,000–$400,000. How much you can get is tied to how much SGLI coverage you have at the time you transition out, however. Additional coverage of $25,000 can be requested on each five-year anniversary up to the maximum coverage available. Premiums, what you pay monthly, quarterly, or annually, are age based. So, as you get older, your premium gets higher.

You can convert your existing SGLI into VGLI within 120 days of separation. If you want to obtain VGLI (without a conversion from SGLI), then you must apply within 240 days of separation or one year and 120 days if you can prove that you're in good health.

Service-Disabled Veterans' Insurance (S-DVI) is also an option. For basic coverage of $10,000, you have to apply within two years from the date you are notified of a service-connected disability. A $20,000 supplemental policy is available if premium payments for the basic policy are waived due to a total disability. If you want the supplemental policy, you have to apply within one year of approval of the waiver of your premiums.

Veterans' Mortgage Life Insurance (VMLI), with a maximum coverage of $200,000, is available to severely disabled veterans who have received grants for specially adapted housing from the VA.

Veterans Pension

The VA helps veterans and their families by providing supplemental income through the Veterans Pension and Survivors Pension benefit programs.

Veterans Pension is a tax-free monetary benefit payable to low-income war-time veterans. Survivors Pension is also tax-free and payable to a low-income, un-remarried surviving spouse and/or unmarried child(ren) of a deceased veteran with wartime service.

> To learn more about any of your potential VA benefits, visit
> www.benefits.va.gov
> or call 1-800-827-1000

Health Care Coverage after Service

The continuation of your health care after life in the military may or may not be an issue for you. Maybe you are going to work directly for a new employer who offers health care benefits and you're covered as a result. Or perhaps you are retiring and have chosen TRICARE Prime, TRICARE Standard, or a commercial health care plan offered by your new employer.

If, however, you do not have some type of coverage in place for that period when you leave the military and do whatever it is you're going to do, then you may want to get some. In this case, you should make it a point to meet with the health benefits advisor at your military treatment facility (MTF). That advisor can tell you all about your options as they relate to your specific situation.

Before you leave the service, it will be to your advantage to get a physical, a dental checkup, and copies of your medical records. Have your family members do the same.

Survivor Benefit Plan (SBP)

If you are retiring from the military, you'll need to decide whether to accept enrollment in the SBP. The SBP is designed to provide ongoing income for your spouse and your minor children, if you should die before them. It pays a monthly annuity up to 55 percent of your retired pay. If you are retiring, you are automatically enrolled in SBP at the time you retire unless you choose to decline SBP. To decline SBP, you will need your spouse's written and notarized concurrence.[9]

PENSION
BENEFITS

WHAT VETERANS AND THEIR FAMILIES SHOULD KNOW WHEN APPLYING FOR DEPARTMENT OF VETERANS AFFAIRS (VA) PENSION BENEFITS

VA's pension program provides monthly benefit payments to certain wartime Veterans with financial need, and their survivors. As Veterans and survivors consider applying for these benefits, VA would like to share important information about the pension program and organizations offering assistance with pension applications.

WHAT ARE PENSION BENEFITS?

- **Pension** is a needs-based benefit paid to a wartime Veteran and his/her survivor(s). A Veteran may generally be eligible if he/she:
  - was discharged from service under other than dishonorable conditions, **AND**
  - served 90 days or more of active military, naval or air service with at least 1 day during a period of war*, **AND**
  - his/her countable income is below the maximum annual pension rate, **AND**
  - meets the net worth limitations, **AND**
  - is age 65 or older, **OR** is shown by evidence to have a permanent and total non-service-connected disability, **OR** is a patient in a nursing home, **OR** is receiving Social Security disability benefits.

  *Veterans who entered active duty after September 7, 1980, must also have served at least 24 months of active duty service. If the total length of service is less than 24 months, the Veteran must have completed his/her entire tour of active duty.

- **Aid and Attendance (A&A)** is an increased monthly pension amount paid to a Veteran or surviving spouse. You may be eligible for the increased A&A amount if:
  - You are eligible for basic pension benefits
    AND
  - You require the aid of another person in order to perform activities of daily living, such as bathing, feeding, dressing, toileting, adjusting prosthetic devices, or protecting yourself from the hazards of your daily environment, **OR**
  - You are bedridden, in that your disability or disabilities require that you remain in bed apart from any prescribed course of convalescence or treatment, **OR**

U.S. Department
of Veterans Affairs

- o You are a patient in a nursing home due to mental or physical incapacity, **OR**
- o You have corrected visual acuity of 5/200 or less, in both eyes, or concentric contraction of the visual field to 5 degrees or less.

- **Housebound** is an increased monthly pension amount paid to a Veteran or surviving spouse who is substantially confined to his or her home because of permanent disability. You may be eligible if:
  - o You are eligible for basic pension benefits *AND*
  - o You have a single permanent disability evaluated as 100-percent disabling **AND**, due to a disability or disabilities, you are permanently and substantially confined to your immediate premises, **OR**
  - o You have a single permanent disability evaluated as 100-percent disabling **AND** another disability or disabilities, independently evaluated as 60-percent or more disabling.

What do I need to know about the organizations that are offering assistance with claims for pension benefits?

- **The U.S. Senate Special Committee on Aging** (Committee) found that some organizations are misrepresenting themselves while helping Veterans and survivors apply for VA pension.
  - o In a June 2012 hearing, the Committee addressed concerns that some organizations are marketing financial products and services to enable claimants whose assets exceed the VA pension program's financial eligibility thresholds to qualify for VA pension benefits.
  - o The Committee also learned these organizations may charge substantial fees for products and services that may not always be in claimants' best long-term interests.
  - o You can access a video of the hearing on the Committee's website.

- **The U.S. Government Accountability Office** (GAO) published a report, Veterans' Pension Benefits: Improvements Needed to Ensure Only Qualified Veterans and Survivors Receive Benefits, GAO-12-540. GAO found that:
  - o There are over 200 organizations that market financial and estate-planning services to help pension claimants with excess assets meet financial eligibility requirements for pension benefits.
  - o These organizations consist primarily of financial planners and attorneys who offer products such as annuities and trusts.
  - o Some products and services provided, such as annuities, may not be suitable for elderly Veterans because they may not have access to all their funds for their care within their expected lifetime without facing high withdrawal fees.
  - o These products and services may result in ineligibility for Medicaid for a period of time.
  - o Some organizations charged fees, ranging from a few hundred dollars for benefits counseling to $10,000 for establishment of a trust.

Who can help me file a claim for VA pension, including pension at the aid and attendance or housebound rates?

- An individual generally must first be accredited by VA to assist a claimant in the preparation, presentation, and prosecution of a claim for VA benefits—even without charge. VA accredits three types of individuals for this purpose:
    - Representatives of VA-recognized Veterans service organizations
    - Independent claims agents
    - Private Attorneys

- A searchable list of accredited representatives, agents, and attorneys is available at the VA Office of the General Counsel website: http://www.va.gov/ogc/apps/accreditation/index.asp

- VA accreditation, which is for the sole and limited purpose of preparing, presenting, and prosecuting claims before VA, is necessary to ensure that claimants for VA benefits have responsible, qualified representation.

- VA regulations allow a one-time exception to this general rule, which allows VA to authorize a person to prepare, present, and prosecute one claim without accreditation. The assistance must be without cost to the claimant, is subject to the laws governing representation, and may not be used to evade the accreditation requirements.

- Preparation and presentation of a VA claim includes, among other things, gathering the information necessary to file a claim for benefits, completing claim applications, submitting claim information to VA, and communicating with VA on behalf of a claimant.

- A VA-accredited attorney or claims agent, who is also a financial planner, may assist a claimant with a claim for A&A. However, financial planners may not use their VA accreditation for the purpose of promoting or selling financial products.

- If VA determines that an accredited attorney or agent is using VA accreditation for an improper purpose, VA may suspend or cancel the individual's accreditation.

Can an accredited attorney or claims agent, who is also a financial planner, charge a fee for preparing a claim for A&A?

- No. An accredited attorney or claims agent may generally charge claimants a fee only **after** an agency of original jurisdiction (e.g., a VA regional office) has issued a decision on a claim, a notice of disagreement has been filed, and the attorney or agent has filed a power of attorney and a fee agreement with VA.

- An exception applies when an accredited attorney or claims agent receives a fee or salary from a disinterested third party. A third party is considered disinterested only if the entity or individual would not benefit financially from the successful outcome of the claim.

- We note that some individuals charge a pre-filing "consultation" fee to inform a Veteran or survivor about VA benefits that may be available to them. In certain states, a license to practice law may be required to provide and charge a fee for such "consultations," which may be considered giving legal advice.

- Such "consultation" fees are unlawful if they are charged after a Veteran or survivor becomes a VA **claimant** by expressing to the attorney or agent an intent to file a claim for VA benefits.

- A "consultation" fee may not be tied to the outcome of a claim filed with VA if the attorney or agent provides any claims assistance—that is, an attorney or agent cannot agree to refund the fee if, after the attorney or agent assists with a VA claim, VA ultimately denies the claim. Such a fee would amount to an unlawful contingency fee or advance payment for assistance with an application for VA benefits.

- VA-recognized Veterans service organizations, including their accredited representatives, are not permitted to receive fees for their services in connection with a VA claim in any instance.

- If VA determines that an accredited attorney or agent is improperly charging a fee for preparing, presenting, or prosecuting a claim prior to the filing of a notice of disagreement, VA may suspend or cancel the individual's accreditation.

Is it permissible to offer a guarantee that a claimant will be awarded A&A or that the processing of a claim will be expedited?

- No. Such promises are patently misleading because VA is ultimately the adjudicator of claims for VA benefits.

- If VA determines that an accredited attorney or agent has misled or deceived a claimant regarding benefits or other rights under programs administered by VA, VA may suspend or cancel the individual's accreditation.

BEING FINANCIALLY FIT ENOUGH TO TRANSITION OUT

Transitioning out of the service is hard enough without having to worry how to make ends meet sans a routine paycheck. Of course, if you are retiring, then you will still get one, but understand in advance that it will not be as big as the one you received in uniform. It will only arrive in your bank account once a month and taxes are likely to eat up a portion of it.

When you transition out, those routine paychecks cease to exist until you can replace them with new ones from a new employer, assuming your post-uniform plans involve a second career.

If you planned your military-to-civilian transition accordingly and good fortune played along, then you have a great job and an expected incoming paycheck lined up. Good fortune, however, can be somewhat elusive and fickle at times. You need to prepare for the possibility that she will not be nice to you.

In other words, you need to be financially able to sustain yourself throughout your transition, however long that ends up being.

New Post-Uniform Expenses You May Have to Bear

While you have been serving in uniform, Uncle Sam has taken care of you and your family in many ways.

- You have had a place to live, free of charge on the military installation, or you have been allocated funds to support living off of it.
- You may have received a food allowance or periodic funds to buy new uniforms.
- When you or anyone in your family became sick, you might have gone to the installation clinic to be seen by a doctor or to the dentist for your biannual exam.

When you retire or transition out of uniform, you will not get these exact benefits any longer. If you are retiring, of course, there will be some stream of continuity here in health care, but even that will look, feel, and cost you differently.

As you think about what your life will look like as a civilian, it is important to know that there may be a few new line items appearing on your monthly budget.

Housing Costs

Where will you be living after you get out? Will you be paying a monthly mortgage, homeowner association (HOA) dues, and associated utilities? If you want to live in a good school district for your children or for the resale value of your house, then you are going to pay for it one way or another.

What will you do when the garbage disposal gets clogged up and you have to call a plumber at $135 per hour? Will you have that extra cash on hand to pay for those services? If you own a home, there are property taxes to consider as well.

Even assuming that homeownership is not in the cards at the moment, you will still need to pay rent and utilities.

Medical/Dental Care

Depending on how you transition out of service, you may already have continued health care benefits lined up. If you are retiring, certainly you have the option to continue coverage under one of the TRICARE programs. (See www.Tricare.mil for more information.) Don't think that this coverage comes free of charge. There may be premiums and copays involved, and rates of those payments are subject to change.

If you have been keeping up with the news, then you know that there is an ever-continuing push within Congress to mandate far-reaching changes in the Military Health System. In other words, Congress (and the DoD) is trying to figure out how to put more of the financial responsibility of health care back onto retirees. Do not be surprised to see enrollment fees where there were none and initiatives limiting coverage in some instances.

If you are not retiring, but you are separating from service with an honorable discharge, then you may have the option to continue coverage for a limited period of time. Again, it will cost you out of pocket to do so.

Other New Costs You Might Incur

In addition to housing and health care costs, you might find yourself shelling out the bucks for federal and state taxes, your own professional wardrobe, transportation costs, renter's or homeowner's insurance, life insurance, disability insurance, or even long-term-care insurance. You won't be receiving any food allowances from Uncle Sam, either. If you're retiring, you may still be able to shop at the commissary, but even then, expect higher prices due to ongoing reforms. If you have children who will require child care services, factor that in as well.

Establish and Contribute to a Transition Budget

Finding a good job can take time.

On the average, it could take anywhere between three and six months to land a civilian job, conservatively speaking. If you are targeting a federal job, it could take much longer, even up to a year. (In that case, you may want to consider alternative employment until you get in the federal system.)

In the meantime, bills still need to be paid and your family still has to eat. A transition budget can help see you through this time period. When you attend the TAP, they will show you how to create one.

Figure Out Your Post-Uniform Salary Range

Not only do you want to be able to pay the bills, have a roof over your head, and eat while you're transitioning out, but you also want to be able to focus on getting a job with a good salary.

When you think about what you could make in your next job, you probably want to earn at least as much as you're making now. Ideally, you may want to earn even more.

To come up with that realistic target salary range, you have to take into consideration a number of factors and do your research.

One of the biggest factors to consider is you. What specific skills do you have to offer an employer? What level within an organization are you targeting? Are you expecting to go from one position of leadership and management straight into another one? Or are you targeting a different professional level? Maybe even a technical level?

Where are you willing to work, geographically? This will play a big role in what your salary expectations are. For example, if you want to target a job in Washington, DC, you're going to have a higher salary range than if you were targeting a similar job in Colorado Springs, Colorado, because of the cost of living index.

When you think about setting a realistic salary range, your skills and the location you are targeting aren't the only factors to consider, although they are big ones.

You have to also keep in mind the differences you may experience between military and civilian compensation. Because of the differences between taxes and benefits, it's entirely possible that your new take-home pay will be less than what you were used to in the military.

In the military you may have enjoyed a number of allowances that were not taxed by the federal government such as a housing allowance, combat pay, an overseas cost of living allowance, and/or a monthly subsistence. In the civilian or federal workforce, you may not get comparable allowances, and even if you do, they may not be tax-free. It depends on who you work for, where you're working, and what employers offer you. It's in your best interest to compensate for those allowances as you establish your post-uniform salary range.

In the military, your medical and dental bills were covered by simply showing someone your ID card at the front desk at the installation clinic. You pay them (or at least the insurance premiums, copays, and deductibles) as a civilian. Even if you retire from service, you still pay something.

If you require child care in your household, you may have to consider the high cost of that as a civilian, too.

We will discuss how to set your salary range and negotiate salaries in more detail in chapter 4, "Job Hunting 101."

Financial Tips to Help You Transition Well

- Establish a transition budget.
- Do your best to eliminate or pay down any debt.
- Get a copy of your credit report and understand what it tells you. Know your credit score and how that could potentially affect you, one way or another. For example, potential employers may check your credit report before they offer you a job, and banks will certainly want to know if you are likely to pay them back before they loan you money for a house or a car.
- Understand how your current tax liability will differ from your future one. Chances are good that you will owe more taxes. You may also be available for a variety of veteran-related tax breaks within your state.
- Circle April 15 on your calendar and note it as the IRS deadline for paying any taxes owed.
- Select your home of record carefully. Consult with legal services regarding the financial and legal pros and cons.

- Make sure you have an adequate amount of commercial life insurance just in case the worst should happen.
- Don't forget about your TSP. You can leave the funds in it (but not add anything else to it), roll them over into a traditional IRA, or roll them over into your new employer's plan. Be sure you understand any fees involved before you do. You can also cash out your TSP, but that will cost you dearly in taxes and penalties, and it defeats the purpose of retirement savings. Visit https://www.tsp.gov for more information.
- Establish and grow an emergency fund (if you haven't already done so).
- If you are physically moving from one location to another, be sure you keep your home address updated in the process.
- Revisit and revise your existing budget as you go along.
- Create a long-term strategy for financial success. Consider working with a certified financial planner.
- Stay healthy or get healthy. Healthy people generally don't have excess and costly health care expenses to deal with.
- Take advantage of your VA benefits. (Read more about them earlier in this chapter.)
- When you do become employed outside of the military, review the income tax withholding on your new pay. If you don't do that correctly and your pay is significantly higher than it was while you were in uniform, you could find yourself owing a lot of money next April 15.

4

Job Hunting 101

Practical Tips to Help You Get Hired

Sooner or later, you are going to have to jump into the job search process and begin the hard work of finding your next job.

You may not be looking forward to it. It is, after all, a new kind of landscape for you. You may be used to being assigned your jobs. It is different now. You have to go out, compete for it, and win it.

Finding a job, though, will not be as hard today as it was a few years ago.

According to the U.S. Department of Labor (DoL), recent statistics out of the Bureau of Labor Statistics (BLS) indicate that the unemployment rate for veterans is at 3.9 percent, down from 4.5 percent in 2016.[1] This is particularly good news for you if you consider that the unemployment rate for veterans aged eighteen to twenty-four reached 29 percent in 2011.[2]

In the last decade, there has been a great effort to help you and your family members find meaningful employment in your post-uniform life. You can perhaps credit a good portion of that decrease in the unemployment rate to the hard work of many unnamed advocates, including policymakers within the Departments of Defense and Labor; trailblazers in Hiring Our Heroes, an initiative of the U.S. Chamber of Commerce; and researchers within the Institute for Veterans and Military Families, to name only a few. You can thank the countless organizational and individual voices that advocated on your behalf. You can also thank the unsung service provider heroes in transition assistance offices throughout the world who gave you preseparation briefings, VA benefits briefing, and job search assistance classes.

Still, when you are unemployed (or soon to be), statistics, even good ones, are of little comfort. You are more focused on what *your* next step is going to be and wondering whether it is the right step to move you forward in your career and in this next chapter of your life.

In other words, things just got real. Am I right?

To face real, you have to be prepared. That is what this chapter is about, and it all starts with you being in the right frame of mind to get your job search started.

CLARIFY YOUR INITIAL JOB SEARCH EXPECTATIONS

Forethought and careful planning is beneficial to you before you transition out of service, and it is equally beneficial to you before you start your job search.

In other words, do the necessary work inside your head before you start anything. You want to be able to clearly identify at the outset what matters the most to you in your job search.

If you don't take the time to do this first and feel confident about it, then you could eventually lose your way. When that happens, you are more likely to make bad decisions along the way and end up working in a job that doesn't fit you.

Define Your Priorities

It helps to establish and/or review your job search priorities before you start writing a resume, applying for jobs, and so on.

So ask yourself the question and answer it: *What matters the most to you?*

Is it imperative that you find a new job in a specific location? Is the job itself the most important aspect of your search, or are you in it for the money?

For example, assume that you felt *job location* was your highest priority before you started your search. You have to remember that fact because, if you don't, fate will hand you a job offer in a different location with a signifi-cantly higher salary.

Fate likes to watch you squirm.

If job location is truly your first priority in that case and staying true to it is important, then you know how to respond to the employer's offer: *Thanks, but no thanks.* Who is squirming now, fate?

However, priorities can and do change all the time. In the above case, you might be tempted to say "to heck with job location parameters." You are taking the job with the big bucks and will just have to console yourself by buying a nicer car and taking a bigger vacation.

Is it okay to flip-flop on your own priorities once you have set them?

It is if you say it is. People often start out wanting one ideal and accepting a different one as time goes by. It is not necessarily a bad thing, and it may just mean that you are being flexible, which leads us to the next topic.

Determine Your Flexibility Factor

Flexibility is a useful tool in your job search and a beautiful concept in life if you want to push the envelope of being philosophical.

How flexible are you going to be here in your job search? Are you willing to pack up and move to the far ends of the earth for the right job? Are you determined to find professional fulfillment within a fifty-mile radius?

The quantity and perhaps even the quality of job opportunities offered to you could differ significantly depending on your answer.

Simply put, the more flexible you are in your job search, the more likely you are to find a good job in relatively short order.

Determine Your Marketability Factor

In addition to your flexibility factor, you might want to consider your *marketability* factor. You may know what you want to do professionally in this brave new world, and an abundance of kudos to you for having such vision. Is there, however, a market for your skills, factoring in your flexibility quotient?

You can be the best baker in the world, but if your target market is already saturated with other bakers, then you might have a marketability problem. If that happens to you, the solution lies in expanding your area of consideration, which could mean revising your priorities. Flexibility to the rescue once again . . .

Determine Your Desired Salary Range

Before you ever set foot in a job interview, you should have a good idea of your acceptable salary range. While the topic of salary may not come up in your first job interview (and you certainly shouldn't mention it, either), you should still know what range you are targeting.

How do you get to that range? It is not easy, truthfully.

Comparing military pay with civilian pay can be problematic because, as you know all too well, military and civilian jobs can be quite different.

In the civilian world of work, you go to work, put in your hours, and go home at the end of the day or at the end of your shift, unless, of course, you work in a career similar to the military such as law enforcement or emergency services.

Tomorrow, or so the theory goes, is another day. Anything you didn't finish today can be taken care of then. You will get a paycheck regardless.

If you are required to work overtime, you have no worries. That just means you get paid on a time-and-a-half basis on evenings and weekends and double-time basis on holidays. Cha-ching.

Your civilian employer may offer you internal advancement opportunities, sick leave, and even a week or two of vacation time once you have worked there long enough.

If you have chosen well, then your job may come with excellent benefits, such as medical, dental, vision, 401(k), educational assistance, and assorted other perks.

In the military world of work, things operate a little differently.

You put in the hours, and you may or may not go home at the end of the day. It doesn't matter. You are always on the clock. You get a bimonthly paycheck (unless Congress goes rogue again), but it doesn't reflect any overtime even though you may have had plenty.

If you are like the majority of service members, you have tax-free benefits including a housing allowance, food allowance, clothing allowance, health care, and other unique special pays and incentives along the way, depending on where you are stationed and what you happen to be doing at the time.

You also get thirty days of paid vacation annually, assuming you are not deployed in some war zone getting shot at. (Note to self: You will miss getting thirty days of paid vacation.)

If you catch a cold, you typically man up and drive on. Unless, of course, you have doctor's orders in hand, cutting you an iota of slack, but even then, you are still on call.

The differences in military and civilian jobs are real. The fact remains that you want your post-uniform job to pay at least, if not more than, what your military job paid.

In theory, you want to move up—not down—the career ladder. To make sure you are targeting the right jobs within an appropriate salary range, know your salary range.

To easily figure out your salary range, access any number of online calculators. Here are a few good options:

Regular Military Compensation Calculator (http://militarypay.defense.gov/Calculators/RMC-Calculator/)

Military Officers Association of America (MOAA) (http://www.moaa.org/calculators/MilitaryPay.html)

G.I. Jobs Military to Civilian Pay Calculator (http://www.gijobs.com/military-pay-calculator/)

WHERE YOU MIGHT FIND YOUR NEXT JOB

It is not enough to know that you want a good job. Everyone who is out there pimping his resume wants a good job. The big question is: How are you going to get it? Where are you going to concentrate your efforts in your job search?

If you focus on a specific type of job and/or a specific industry, then you narrow your search efforts, presumably on an area that is the best fit for your skills and abilities. That is a good place to start. You can always expand your job search efforts if what you are doing isn't working.

What Are Your Obvious Options?

Do you see yourself remaining in the DoD family but working in a different role, perhaps as a federal employee or a civilian contractor? You certainly wouldn't be the first one to take off your uniform, put on a suit, and walk through the same door you walked out of when you transitioned out of the military. Or maybe you want to continue working in the federal government but not the DoD. There are ample government departments and agencies to choose from. You could also turn your attention to working for state government or city management.

Or are you ready for a cultural break and seek employment outside of the DoD and, indeed, outside of the government altogether in the private industry or nonprofit world?

Maybe none of these options appeal to you. Could you perhaps be leaning toward small-business ownership? Do you see yourself as the owner of a franchise?

The point is simple. You have options—many of them. Figure out one or two areas, at least to begin with, that you want to put the lion's share of your efforts into as you launch your search efforts.

Where the Demand Is

It may help you to figure out where you want to put your initial efforts if you know which jobs are the fastest growing. The fastest-growing occupations, per the DoL,[3] are listed in table 4.1.

Table 4.1. Twenty Fastest-Growing Occupations

Occupation	Growth Rate (%)	Median Annual Pay ($)
Wind turbine service technicians	108	51,050
Occupational therapy assistants	43	57,870
Physical therapy assistants	41	55,170
Physical therapy aides	39	25,120
Home health aides	38	21,920
Commercial drivers	37	50,470
Nurse practitioners	35	98,190
Physical therapists	34	84,020
Statisticians	34	80,110
Ambulance drivers/attendants	33	23,740
Occupational therapy aides	31	27,800
Physician assistants	30	98,180
Operations research analysts	30	78,630
Personal financial advisors	30	89,160
Cartographers/photogrammetrists	29	61,880
Genetic counselors	29	72,090
Interpreters/translators	29	44,190
Audiologists	29	74,890
Hearing aid specialists	27	49,600
Optometrists	27	103,900

Source: Occupational Outlook Handbook, December 17, 2015

Another point to consider, as you plot and plan your future, is the longevity factor of your preferred career field. Will what you do be sticking around for the long term, or is it likely to be obsolete in the future? You may not have a crystal ball, but you do want to think about where this first job out of uniform could lead you professionally in a few years. Is there a surface path that makes sense?

You might also want to note, in an effort to avoid tunnel vision and limiting your job possibilities, that you may have highly portable skills that can be employed across a variety of industries. If you are an IT specialist, you can work for anyone with an IT department (which would be just about every industry).

Develop Your Own List of Potential Employers

In an effort to identify potential leads for yourself, consider creating your own list of potential employers. If you have a specific industry pegged, it will be easier to do this. For example, if you would like to work as a defense contractor, then your list may look like this one:

Top 20 Defense Contractors

1	Lockheed Martin	www.lockheedmartin.com
2	Boeing	www.boeing.com
3	BAE Systems	www.baesystems.com
4	Raytheon	www.raytheon.com
5	General Dynamics	www.generaldynamics.com
6	Northrop Grumman	www.northropgrumman.com
7	Airbus	www.airbus.com
8	Leonardo Spa	www.leonardocompany.com/en
9	L-3 Communications	www.l-3com.com
10	Thales	www.thalesgroup.com/en
11	Almaz-Antey	www.almaz-antey.ru/en
12	Huntington Ingalls Industries	www.huntingtoningalls.com
13	United Technologies Corporation	www.utc.com
14	Rolls-Royce	www.rolls-royce.com
15	Honeywell	www.honeywell.com
16	United Aircraft Corporation	www.uacrussia.ru
17	Harris	www.harris.com
18	Textron	www.textron.com
19	GE Aviation	www.geaviation.com
20	Babcock International	www.babcockinternational.com

Source: Extracted from *Defense News*, "Top 100 for 2016," http://people.defensenews.com/top-100/

If you want to work for the federal government, then check out the agencies listing at www.usajobs.gov to create your list of potential employers, review, and apply for job openings.

Private Industry and Nonprofit Jobs

If you are more interested in working within private industry, consider your geographic preferences and develop your list of top twenty employers from that area. The chamber of commerce in your selected area may be a big help in identifying top employers in the area as well as those planning to relocate into it. Just Google "top employers in [wherever]," and chances are you'll be rewarded with a starting point. Most employers will post currently available positions on their website in a section titled "Careers," "Job Opportunities," "Employment," or "Job Openings."

Of course, you can also access any number of mega job boards such as:

www.Indeed.com

www.Monster.com

www.CareerBuilder.com

www.Dice.com

www.Glassdoor.com

www.Idealist.com

www.SimplyHired.com

www.us.jobs.com

You can post your own resume to these sites and apply for jobs. You may get a few leads or even a job. Realize that you aren't the only one using these sites, though. Because of the massive volume of resumes posted, there is the possibility that your efforts may not bring you any significant leads at all. You may begin to receive some new junk mail, however.

What, then, is the point of them?

You can use the big boards to do research on employers (what kind of jobs they are hiring for and where they are filling the jobs). You can also use them to find out what skills are required for different jobs and, equally important, what kind of industry terminology applies. Just like the military had its own language, industries outside of the military have their own lingo as well. If you want to compete for those jobs, you have to understand their language.

Finally, knowing where to send your resume or to apply for jobs is important. You will increase your chances of getting someone's genuine attention if you know who to send it to. (See the next section for more information.)

USING NETWORKING AND SOCIAL MEDIA EFFECTIVELY

Networking is probably something you do all the time; you just didn't call it that. It is relationship building, pure and simple. You used it in the military. You will continue to use it as a civilian. You give. You take. Everybody wins.

Information is power, and networking allows you to be powerful and to help others be powerful. It allows you to connect with real people in a meaningful way.

Networking is crucial all the time, but it is particularly important in your job search.

If you mistakenly think networking is equivalent to sucking up to others and using them for your own selfish purposes, then you aren't tracking here at all. Even if you do understand it, let us review now because of its importance in your job search.

Networking is where you will find the majority of jobs out there. Of course, vacancies appear all the time online on company websites, in newspapers, and in trade journals, but many more jobs are filled before they even get announced. They are filled through networking efforts. You may not like the reality of it, but who you know does make a difference.

Networking is a key component to your career success whether you are actively looking for a job or you are gainfully employed and trying to grow and nourish your career. It is the process of exchanging information, ideas, contract, and referrals, with the key word being *exchanging*.

You network with people you already know, and you expand your network by meeting new people along the way. Anyone can be helpful, regardless of where they work. When you network with someone, you are potentially reaching out not only to that person but also to the people that person knows.

How Can You Effectively Network?

If you want networking to work for you, you have to get your brave on and put yourself out there. You have to be able to effectively engage with others and coherently string a few sentences together. You can do that, right?

It will help if you are comfortable talking about yourself. For example, you have to be able to explain to others what kind of job you are seeking and why you are qualified for it. You have to be able to talk about your past accomplishments in a way that communicates your expertise without sounding arrogant in the process.

For your job search purposes, plan to network both online (using social media to expand your network and increasing your opportunities for employment) and off-line (connecting online identities with real off-line people).

Tips for Networking Online

Like it or not, social media plays an ever-growing role in your job search. Embrace it you must. Nearly half of job seekers surveyed—48 percent—claim they used social media to get their current job.[4]

Through laptops, desktop computers, and mobile phones, job seekers flock to Twitter (17 percent), LinkedIn (20 percent), and Facebook (21 percent)[5] in an effort to connect with others who may be able to give them leads, interviews, or even outright jobs.

Of course, it is not only job seekers surfing online for their next employer. About 92 percent of employment recruiters are also online checking potential candidates out.[6] They're looking for you in all the places you're flocking to above, including your Instagram account.

Top Military-Focused Recruiters

Bradley-Morris, Inc. (BMI)
www.bradley-morris.com

Lucas Group
www.lucasgroup.com

Orion International
www.orioninternational.com

Cameron-Brooks
www.cameron-brooks.com

Alliance
www.alliance-careers.com

With job seekers and employers both in the business of prescreening one another, it makes sense to pay attention to your online persona.

In other words, if you were an employer and you searched yourself online, would you want to interview yourself, or would you wipe the glistening sweat from your furrowed brow, thankful to have dodged a beer-guzzling, Speedo-wearing, foulmouthed, political rant maniac bullet?

First impressions, it would appear, no longer happen in the job interview. They happen online, and you need to make sure your first impression is a good one.

The following tips may help you:

- *Find yourself.* Google your name and see what turns up. You might be shocked to see that you're not the only you out there. Perhaps you could be confused with an East Coast real estate agent, a dead body, or a lawyer. *It happens.* If you want to see exactly how many of you there are without clicking through thousands of pages, visit www.howmanyofme.com. It's positively enlightening.
- *Analyze what you have already published about yourself.* Look through any social media accounts, websites, or blogs you call your own and vet yourself. If you were an employer, would you like what you see, or would you be hesitant to take the budding relationship to the next level?
- *Clean up any potential messes or missteps.* If you have been online for a number of years now, you've grown up. Has your content kept pace with your own personal growth? Maybe it's time to save those crazy half-clothed, bad-haired pictures from your carefree youth on an external drive and delete them from the inquiring eyes of the world at large. Go through your posts and comments, too. Delete the late-night, alcohol-impassioned rants about politics, religion, your Aunt Betty, and all things sports. Also think about the thoughts and words you have expressed online in comparison

with the employers that you are targeting. Do your stated views conflict openly with theirs? That could be a red flag for an employer who is considering calling you up for an interview.

- *Control the message.* After you have deleted the questionable content, tighten up what is left. Certainly do not try to be someone you are not, but put your best digital foot forward. Your reputation is everything, and you need to know what others perceive it to be. If you are concerned that your online identity can be too easily confused with someone else, then differentiate your identity by adding a professional headshot or including your middle initial in your name on all your sites.
- *Monitor your continued presence.* Do not go to all the effort of getting your online presence the way you want it only to ignore it later. Periodically, go through the "Google yourself" process and make sure things are still being presented the way you want them to online. You can also set up a Google Alert, so that anytime your name appears somewhere online, you will get an e-mail telling you about it.

Using Social Media to Nourish and Grow Your Network

Now that you have a not-offensive-in-any-way identity working for you, then it is time to start networking online for your next job.

Start Using LinkedIn Today

If you are not using LinkedIn (www.linkedin.com) yet, today is a good day to start. If you are not familiar with using LinkedIn, don't worry. The site offers easy-to-understand tips for getting started in its Help section. Read it.

At the very least, you want to create a LinkedIn profile to showcase who you are and what you have to offer. Consider joining and actually participating in targeted LinkedIn groups as well. This will help you to build connections and learn the civilian lingo of your chosen industry.

Industry-Specific Blogs, Facebook, and Twitter

While LinkedIn is great, it is not the only way you can connect with others online. Find and contribute to blogs that pertain to the industry you are targeting. (Just Google "[target industry] blogs." It is that easy.) Use Facebook and Twitter, too, if you are comfortable doing so.

You may be tempted to stay and mingle within veteran and military-centric groups because that is who you are most comfortable being around at this point, but don't be afraid to put your digital toes in unfamiliar waters. That is how you truly begin to grow and expand your professional world.

Wherever cybertravels take you, communicate clearly and professionally, as though you were already being considered for the job you seek.

Networking Off-Line

Social media networking gets all the glory these days, but you cannot underestimate the power of face-time networking with others.

Online networking is key to establishing a virtual identity. It allows others to put a picture with a name. Off-line networking, however, breathes life into that picture, morphing it into a real face.

So how can you do it? Here are some ideas you can use:

- Volunteer in the community for the greater good and meet others of the same mind-set that way.
- Join professional industry-specific associations and become an active member.
- Go to local chamber of commerce networking events.
- Have basic business cards with you at all times so you can exchange them with others if the situation arises.
- Have a prepared "elevator pitch" ready to use in any situation.
- Don't sound like a shady used car salesperson trying to make the monthly quota before the end of the business day. Listen thoughtfully and think before you speak.
- Try to truly connect with the person you're talking with, and remember, it's a two-way conversation.
- Begin with the mind-set of "What can I do for this person?" rather than the other way around.
- Be yourself.

Major bonus points to those who can effectively and geographically network off-line with those they have met online.

THE THREE BASIC TOOLS YOU NEED FOR YOUR JOB SEARCH

Anytime you start a big job, you want to be sure you have all the right tools assembled to help you achieve your goal.

Your job search is no different. While you will revise things along the way to better address the given set of circumstances, you can always start with a basic set of tools.

In this case, the essential tools are your resume(s), a cover letter, and an elevator pitch. There are other tools that you may find useful as well, such as a list of professional references and a portfolio of your work if that is deemed relevant to the type of job you are targeting.

Essential Tool #1: Your Resume

A resume is a document that communicates your work history and qualifications to an employer. It is a necessary evil in the job search process.

Contrary to popular belief, resumes alone are not responsible for getting you hired. They can be instrumental, however, in securing a job interview, at which point you can impress the employer and ideally land the job.

Resumes are quite important, and you will want to have one (or two) ready to adapt and roll out as needed. As you probably learned in your Transition Assistance Program class (or you will learn when you do go), the kind of resume you need depends on what kind of job you are applying for.

For example, if you want to apply for a federal job, then you will need a federal resume. A federal resume typically runs about four to six pages long and gets into way more detail than you can imagine. By contrast, if you want to apply for a job with a defense contractor or with a civilian employer, then you will need a basic one- to two-page resume.

One Resume Isn't Enough

One resume alone will not work for all the jobs you apply for. Accept that cold hard fact right now. If you want to be seriously considered for the next step (i.e., a job interview), then you need to spend ample time preparing a quality written product that effectively highlights your qualifications and experiences as they pertain to the job in question.

Another reality to keep in mind here is that there is no one right way to create a resume. There are many different ways you can format one and present it.

The right way is the one that best showcases what you have to offer and marries it effectively with the job you want.

What Type of Resume Do You Need?

There are many types of resumes to choose from, and it is not the goal of this book to overwhelm you on the subject. Rather, this book is intended to give you the basic skills you need to hit the job search path running. To that end, let us discuss three (and only three) basic formats that will work well for you in three common situations. (You're welcome.)

Situation One: You are seeking a job as a civilian doing the same or similar job you did while in uniform. You have a consistent work history that shows career progression.

A Good Bet: You can't go wrong with a basic chronological resume, which focuses on your most recent work experience and works itself back about ten years. This is the easiest resume format to create, too.

Situation Two: You are tired of doing what you did in uniform and want to do something new.

A Good Bet: A combination (combo) format resume might work for you in this case. A combo format does an excellent job of showcasing transferrable skills and qualifications accumulated over a period of time while de-emphasizing (but not excluding) your work history. The secret to this format's success lies in the placement of information.

Situation Three: You want to apply for a federal job.

A Good Bet: A detailed keyword-structured resume, incorporating specific keywords from the job vacancy announcement and providing examples of required skills noted on the supplemental occupational questionnaire, works best here.

Essential Tool #2: A Cover Letter

Cover letters, some experts suggest, are becoming antiquated in the job search. That is just not true unless you consider clear communications a thing of the past.

A cover letter, whether it is a literal letter accompanying the paper version of your resume or a message crafted within the confines of an e-mail, provides a framework of reference for what comes next—namely, the resume.

Chronological Resume Template

Your Name Here
Your Address, Telephone Number, and E-mail Address on This Line

SUMMARY OF QUALIFICATIONS

In this section, either as a paragraph or as a bulleted list, include 7–10 key points that highlight your skills, abilities, and qualifications as they relate to the job you are applying for with this particular version of your resume.

PROFESSIONAL WORK HISTORY

JOB TITLE   **Year to Year**
Employer Name and Address

[In this format of resume, you are providing the employer with a chronological history of your employment, starting with the most recent job you've held in service and working back in time. Chronological resumes generally cover a 7- to 10-year period.]

JOB TITLE   **Year to Year**
Employer Name and Address

[It is important to communicate your skills on this resume (and on any resume, for that matter) in a way so that the reader will understand you. In other words, translate military lingo that may be lost on someone outside the DoD.]

JOB TITLE   **Year to Year**
Employer Name and Address

[In this section, provide your work history with dates. You don't have to give exact dates of employment unless the employers specifically instruct you to do so. Instead of using the Year-to-Year format, you could also use Month/Year to Month/Year. Whatever format you opt to use with one entry, keep it consistent with the remaining entries.]

EDUCATION AND TRAINING

- Academic Degree, Area of Concentration, University, Year Graduated
- Certificate, Military Course, Branch of Service, Year Completed

[In this section, list your most relevant academic and military training chronologically, with the most recent first. Start with the academics, listing highest degree first. After you provide your academic achievements, list the relevant military training you have accomplished. Do not list every military course you have ever taken in your career. Avoid including training that happened more than 10 years ago. It is okay to translate military-sounding course titles if you do not think they are easily understandable to someone outside the military.]

PROFESSIONAL AFFILIATIONS

[In this section, list the relevant professional organizations you belong to.]

Combination Resume Template

Your Name Here

Your Address, Telephone Number, and E-mail Address on This Line

SUMMARY OF QUALIFICATIONS

In this section, either as a paragraph or as a bulleted list, include 7–10 key points that highlight your skills, abilities, and qualifications as they relate to the job you are applying for with this particular version of your resume.

AREAS OF EXPERTISE

SKILL AREA #1

[In this type of resume, you are emphasizing your skills and abilities over your work history. It is a good format to use if you are changing career gears or if you want to highlight older but still relevant experiences.]

SKILL AREA # 2

[Instead of separating your work history chronologically here, you are synthesizing your primary skill areas over the life (or the last 7–10 years of it, anyway) of your career.]

SKILL AREA # 3

[In this example, only three Skill Areas are outlined. You can have more of them, however. If you need an additional page, just include your name and Page 2 at the top of the second page and continue on. You do not need to repeat the entire heading.]

PROFESSIONAL WORK HISTORY

JOB TITLE   **Year to Year**
Employer Name and Address

JOB TITLE   **Year to Year**
Employer Name and Address

JOB TITLE   **Year to Year**
Employer Name and Address

[In this section, provide your work history. You don't have to give exact dates of employment unless the employers specifically tell you to do so. Instead of using the Year-to-Year format, you could also use Month/Year to Month/Year. Whatever format you opt to use with one entry, keep it consistent with the remaining entries.]

EDUCATION AND TRAINING

- Academic Degree, Area of Concentration, University, Year Graduated
- Certificate, Military Course, Branch of Service, Year Completed

[In this section, list your most relevant academic and military training chronologically, with the every military course you have ever taken in your career. Avoid including training that happened more than 10 years ago. It is okay to translate military-sounding course titles if you do not think they are easily understandable to someone outside the military.]

PROFESSIONAL AFFILIATIONS

[In this section, list the relevant professional organizations you belong to. If you hold a leadership position in them, say so.]

Federal Resume Template

YOUR NAME HERE

CONTACT INFORMATION

In this section, show your current address, telephone number, and e-mail address.

SUMMARY OF QUALIFICATIONS

In this section, either as a paragraph or as a bulleted list, include 7–10 key points that highlight your skills, abilities, and qualifications as they relate to the job you are applying for with this particular federal resume.

CORE COMPETENCIES

In this section, list the key skill areas that you have, by title only, (1) that are important to the job you are applying for and (2) that best support the job, whether a perfect match or not. You can display the skill titles in a column here, providing visual layout appeal and saving precious resume space at the same time. If you have a DoD security clearance, list it here too.

WORK HISTORY

JOB TITLE   **Month/Year to Month/Year**
Employer   Hours worked per week: 40
Street Address, City, State
Supervisor: Name, telephone, or e-mail address. Indicate if okay for direct contact.

KEYWORD SKILL AREA. The keyword skill areas that you discuss here, assuming they most support the job you are applying for, should also appear as Core Competencies above. You will want to elaborate here about your expertise and experience with the skill as you gleaned it from the job itself.

KEYWORD SKILL AREA. It will also be helpful, as you craft your federal resume, to refer to the required skills on the job vacancy announcement and within the supplemental occupational questionnaire. In fact, you will want to directly address that required knowledge, those skills and abilities in some detail here. Your resume **must** support your answers to that questionnaire, and to the job requirements noted on the vacancy announcement. If it doesn't, or if it is not written strong enough, then you will probably not be rated among the best qualified and referred for the job. The truth hurts. Take your time with this document and get it right.

KEYWORD SKILL AREA. Ideally, you will have 3–5 (or even a couple more) keyword skill area paragraphs. Your federal resume will most likely run between 4 and 6 pages. That's okay. Don't let it run to 10 or 20 pages. That is too long. While you may have ample professional experience to showcase, you must be selective in what you present. It must be relative, relative, relative.

EDUCATION AND SPECIALIZED TRAINING

-
- Academic Degree, Area of Concentration, University, Year Graduated
- Certificate, Military Course, Branch of Service, Year Completed

[In this section, list your most relevant academic and military training chronologically, with the most recent first. Start with the academics, listing highest degree first. After you provide your academic achievements, list the relevant military training you have accomplished. Do not list every military course you have ever taken in your career. Avoid including training that happened more than 10 years ago. It is okay to translate military-sounding course titles if you do not think they are easily understandable to someone outside the military.]

ADDITIONAL INFORMATION

[In this section, you can list anything else that is relevant that does not fit nicely into one of the headers above. For example: alternate contact information, veterans preference for employment, and foreign language abilities.]

Additional Federal Resume Writing Tips

- If you are applying for a federal job in the DoD, chances are that a real person, and not a computer, will be reading your resume to determine whether you are qualified for a given job. Make that reader's life easier by only including relevant information fully explained.

- Other non-DoD agencies and departments, while they post their openings on the same USAJOBS website as the DoD, may have different application processes in place. Don't be surprised to find yourself redirected to their site, rather than hanging out on USAJOBS, when applying for their jobs. Those departments and agencies may also have a real person review resumes or they may not. You can always call the point of contact on the job vacancy announcement to find out in order to target your resume appropriately.

- You don't have to create your own federal resume like this one. You can use the Resume Builder provided on the USAJOBS website too. The same content suggestions given here apply there as well. You can also opt instead to create a basic chronological resume without the keyword approach used here as long as you continue to address the qualifications noted in the job vacancy announcement and in the occupational questionnaire.

- Before you apply for any federal jobs, make sure you are first eligible to apply for them. Then read the job vacancy announcement (and any supplemental information provided) to make sure you are genuinely qualified for the job.

- Networking will help you land a federal job, too.

In other words, a cover letter sets the stage for your resume. It tells the reader, without guesswork, why your resume is in his hands in the first place. If it is written well, it also gives the employer a sneak peek of your own voice and personality, as opposed to the flat voice of a fact-laden document.

Cover letters dead? *Pshaw.*

All you need to know is how to write one. Lucky for you, a basic template follows:

Your Name Here

Your Address, Telephone Number, and E-mail Address on This Line

Date

Name
Job Title
Address
City, State, Zip

Dear Mr. or Mrs. Last Name:

In Paragraph 1: Explain why you are sending the addressee this letter and your resume. If you are applying for a specific job, include the job title and job vacancy number (if applicable). If someone referred you personally, mention that here.

In Paragraph 2: Explain briefly why you are a good fit for the job. Don't repeat your resume word for word, however. If you need an additional paragraph here to show the match between your skills and the qualifications for the job, it should be fine. Try to keep the length of the cover letter to one page only, however. Mention that your resume is enclosed or attached.

In Paragraph 3: Close out the letter. Thank the person you are writing for his or her consideration and mention that you will follow up with that person by a specific day. Make a note on your calendar to do that while you're at it.

Sincerely,

[your signature here if snail mailing the letter]

Your Typed Name Here

Additional Cover Letter Tips

- If you are e-mailing a resume, your cover letter then becomes the content of your e-mail message. Use the same content guidance for what to write in your message, omitting the to address, the date, and the header.

Essential Tool # 3: An Elevator or Sales Pitch

Tell me about yourself.

Someone will eventually say this to you, or else you will have a moment in time when you know you should answer the implied question, whether it was asked or not.

As you network and interview for jobs, you are going to have to speak intelligently and clearly with others about what it is that makes you such a professional catch. This may come easily for some, but not for everyone. If you fall in the latter camp, then you will find the following example of an elevator pitch a useful guide as you create your own.

Tips to keep in mind about this valuable job search tool:

- Keep your pitch short and sweet, to the tune of about thirty to sixty seconds. (You can always develop a lengthier pitch for appropriate situations.)
- The elevator pitch should highlight who you are, what you do well, and your greatest strength or a significant and relative accomplishment. It should also express what it is you want to do and why you want to do it.
- Practice your pitch before you actually use it. You want it to sound natural, like you are having a conversation, and not stilted, like you are trying to remember your next line.

INTERVIEWING AND SALARY NEGOTIATING SKILLS

Sooner or later, you will find yourself invited to a job interview. This means you are doing something right, and you certainly want to keep doing things right so that you ultimately get a job offer.

Prepare for the Interview in Advance

- Know what job you are being interviewed for and who will be interviewing you.
- Learn as much as you can about this would-be employer by reading the company website and by searching for them online in current business news.
- Know where the interview will take place and figure out when you need to leave point A to get there in plenty of time, taking into consideration traffic and other obstacles.
- Study up on civilian vocabulary words so you can use them from this point forward. Each industry has its own lingo. You are fluent in DoD. Now you need to be fluent in the language of the civilian industry. (Hint: Your networking activities, particularly those online through LinkedIn group discussions, can be effective for this purpose.)

What to Do the Day of Your Job Interview

- Arrive for the interview about fifteen minutes early, no sooner and no later.
- Show up looking like you mean business by dressing appropriately for the occasion.

- If you are comfortable doing so, bring along a nice briefcase or portfolio that has extra copies of your resume, a pen, and a pad of paper for note taking.
- If you have to wait around for the interview to begin, launch into intel ops mode. Observe what is going on around you in order to get a feel for how things seem to work there. You, more than anyone, understand that valuable information can be learned by just watching everyone around you.
- When you are called into the interview, be sure you watch your body language in the opening salvo and throughout the course of the meeting. For example, make confident eye contact and shake hands firmly. Don't fidget. Don't cross your arms or your legs so there is a created barrier between you and the employer. You want to appear approachable, confident, and knowledgeable. Check any arrogance or superiority at the door. Those traits won't win you any accolades here.
- Let the employer take the lead in the interview even if he is not all that skilled in the process. This is his party. His job. You are the guest—for now.
- Continue breathing. Breathing is an easy thing to stop doing when you may be nervous or anxious about wanting to make a good impression. If you do not breathe, however, you do not get enough oxygen into your lungs and your mind starts to miss simple things. You want your mind fully engaged here. You want to listen and really hear the comments being made and the questions being asked. *Breathe*.
- When you are asked questions, answer them thoughtfully and in the language that they speak, not military-ese. Ditch the single-syllable answers and briefly elaborate. They want to get to know you. You want to get to know them. There has to be a meaningful conversation if that's going to happen.

Commonly Asked Interview Questions

Questions an Employer Might Ask You

- Tell me about yourself.
- How did you learn about this position?
- What do you know about our company?

- Why are you interested in this particular job?
- What are your strengths? Your weaknesses?
- What achievement are you most proud of in your career to date?
- Where do you see yourself professionally in five years? In ten years?
- Tell me about a time when you failed on the job.
- Why are you leaving your current employer?
- What are you looking for in a job?
- How would former coworkers describe you?
- What is your management style?
- How do you handle pressure and stress on the job?
- What are your salary requirements?
- Why should we hire you?
- When can you start?
- Do you have any questions for us?

Questions You Might Ask an Employer

- How would you describe a typical day on the job?
- Do employees work well together here?
- Is there room for career advancement?
- What is your management style?
- Is this a new position? If so, why?
- Who would be my immediate supervisor?
- How much travel is involved?
- What are the job responsibilities?
- Would I have to relocate for this job at any point?
- Is overtime expected?
- What is the work schedule?
- Does the company promote from within?
- When can I expect to hear from you about this position?
- How has the company changed over the past few years?
- Where would you want me to concentrate my efforts?
- How long have you been with the company, and are you satisfied?
- What qualities does this company most value in its employees?
- When do I start?

- Be prepared to ask your own short list of questions that you may have regarding the job itself, the company, and the culture.
- Be ready to talk salary and benefits in this interview, but don't be the first one to bring up the topic.

Salary Negotiating Tips

- Before you ever walk into a job interview, know your target salary range. Determine your salary range by researching online salary surveys, talking to others who work in your field, or asking a mentor.
- During a job interview, let the employer be the one to bring up the topic of compensation first.
- If you are asked in an interview to tell the employer the salary you are seeking, express your answer in a salary range that is 10 percent above your real salary range versus an exact number. It is easier for you to negotiate down than it is to try to go up.
- Understand that salary isn't the only aspect of the compensation package that can be negotiated. Benefits such as number of vacation days and work schedules can also be discussed.
- Negotiate in person, if possible, and limit the number of points for discussion.
- If you are trying to get the employer to increase the salary offered, give him solid reasons why he should do so.
- If there doesn't appear to be any wiggle room with the salary initially, then try to negotiate the opportunity for a salary increase within a certain period of time, assuming the employer is satisfied with your work performance. Be sure you get this agreement in writing, of course.
- When an offer is made, thank the employer and ask for a day or so to consider it.
- Before you agree to any job offer, get it and the terms associated with it in writing.
- Always keep copies of agreements you have signed for future reference.

- When the interview is winding down and the good-byes are about to be spoken, determine the next steps (assuming the employer hasn't already laid them out for you). Will there be a second or even third interview in the process? When does the employer anticipate making a hiring decision?
- On your exit, thank the employer for his or her time and consideration. Shake hands again, maintaining eye contact and exuding your best "you really want to hire me" charm.
- Soon after the interview (i.e., later that same day or the next morning), craft a thank-you note and send it. You can do this via e-mail or snail mail, but do it. Many job seekers don't do this, and they miss out on a subtle opportunity to (1) show the employer their manners and professionalism, (2) keep their name fresh on the minds of the hiring manager, and (3) say something they neglected to say when they had the chance.
- Soon after the interview (i.e., later that same day), continue your job search. Do not spend precious time hoping that this one job works out at the expense of applying for others. There are so many factors, known and unknown, swirling around in the universe. You cannot afford to pin all your job search hopes on one opportunity. Generate more opportunities, and fast. It is good to have choices in your career.

HOW TO TELL IF IT'S THE RIGHT JOB FOR YOU

You have a job offer. Wonderful. Now all you have to do is figure out whether you want to accept. Unlike military orders, you do have a choice here.

Job Offer Evaluation Checklist

- Can I afford financially to accept this job offer? Is the salary right for me? Can I continue to at least maintain my current standard of living with it?
- Is there an opportunity to advance professionally within the organization and potentially earn more in the future?
- Are all the benefits adequate for my needs and the needs of my family members? (Examples of benefits: medical, dental, vision, educational assistance, personal days, day care, disability insurance, etc.)

- Does the employer offer a good retirement plan? What is it exactly, and how would it complement or combine with my existing retirement plan?
- Are there profit-sharing options as an employee of this company?
- Are there other potential sources of income with this offer, such as a signing bonus or relocation allowance?
- Will I be afforded sick days, personal days, and vacation time? How much annually?
- If I have to travel for the job, will I get reimbursed for that travel, or will they pay for it up front?
- Is the company culture compatible with my own professional and even personal beliefs?
- Does this job/company appear to offer me longevity?

III

MAKING YOUR
NEW NORMAL WORK

Strategies for Success on the New Job

It may seem like the day will never come, but it will. At some point, you will be a civilian, working in a job that does not require a military uniform. You will be, for all intents and purposes, the master of your own universe. *Yay you.*

Whether you are the new boss or simply the newest cog in what may be a very big wheel, people will be watching you, analyzing your every move. They want to see if you will play nicely with others or if you are going to be a problem child to be seriously plotted against.

Are you going to give credence to existing stereotypes about veterans in the workplace? Will you bite first and ask questions later or vice versa? Are you going to be "that guy" who immediately dives in, takes control of what he sees as unacceptable chaos, and smartly reorganizes operations right off the bat? Are you going to be the low-key dude who does nothing but collect a paycheck? Will you be the office wallflower who arrives late, leaves early, and otherwise strives for invisibility? Are you friend or foe?

Inquiring minds want to know, people. How you handle yourself, particularly during the first three months, will tell them everything they need to know, too.

Is it fair that the first one hundred days or so make such a lasting impression? Probably not. After all, this parallel universe represents a whole new world for you. While you're busy finding your way sans uniform, camaraderie, and face paint, your new colleagues will be low-key judging you for who you seem to be at the moment, regardless of whether you even know who that is yourself.

Each organization has its own culture and its own set of written or unwritten rules. It could take some time to figure out what you've gotten yourself into. Until such time that clarity reveals itself to you in all its shining glory, tread lightly, dear warrior. Understand and appreciate that the first one hundred days of being the new kid on the block are crucial days that set the tone for the months and years ahead.

While you can't be expected to know everything on day one, day one is when that first impression is made. Indeed, the next few months on the job, or the first hundred days or so, are when you are going to make an impression on your coworkers and your supervisors, for better or for worse.

The following suggestions are mull-over worthy and may come in handy as you transition from one workplace reality to a new one.

FORTY-FOUR TIPS FOR SURVIVING THE FIRST ONE HUNDRED DAYS

So you want to impress your new boss, make new work friends, and avoid looking like an idiot, right? Here are forty-four tips to help you launch your civilian career and accomplish all those things.

1. Make a Good First Impression

Leadership is already impressed with you, or you would not be working there in the first place. You may or may not be working elbow to elbow with leadership every minute of every day, however. You are going to have to make a good impression on the organizational masses, internally and externally. You can do that by being the kind of colleague you like to work with yourself.

2. Show Up on Time

If anyone knows how to show up on time, it should be you. In the military, if you weren't fifteen minutes early, then you were five minutes late. Apply that same concept to your new job. For example, if the workday is scheduled to run from 8:00 a.m. to 5:00 p.m., show up at 7:45 a.m. By 8:00 a.m., you should be ready to roll workwise.

3. Don't Rush Out the Door at the End of the Day

You might be more than ready to bolt after a hard day of work, but don't be the first one out the door at the end of the day. You will look professionally weak. Instead, plan to arrive fifteen minutes early each day and leave about fifteen minutes after the official quitting time. Use that last quarter hour to organize your tasks for the next day.

4. Leave the Military Lingo in the Past Where It Belongs

You say 0800 hours. Civilians say 8:00 a.m. You say *execute*. Civilians say *implement*. You say *subordinates*. Civilians say *employees*. You get the idea. You came from a world that operated quite effectively using its own unique (and sometimes colorful) language. If you continue to speak that language, don't expect your new colleagues to always understand or even appreciate you. Instead, make a concerted effort to speak English and learn (and use) the language of your new industry.

Don't worry. You'll still get to use acronyms (new ones, of course), and it may be okay to throw in the occasional *hooah* every now and then for old time's sake.

5. Continue to Dress for Success

First face-to-face impressions are important, and you must have made a good one because you were hired. Keep up the good work and remember the tired but true cliché: *Dress a level up from where you want to be professionally.*

6. Keep Learning about Your New Employer

Learn everything you can (that you haven't already learned in the interview process) about your new employer and your new boss. Try to connect the big-picture dots so that you have a good feel for where the company is now, where it's headed in the future, and the degree of influence that your new boss (and potentially you) will have on that projection.

7. Be a Sponge and Don't Try to Make Changes Too Quickly

You may know in your gut that you can make a good thing a hundred times better, and you may be itching to do so. Slow down. You will eventually get your chance. Do not make the critical blunder of being Mr. or Ms. I Know Better Than You Do right out of the new job starting gate.

Instead, channel your inner sponge and absorb everything around you in those first days and weeks. Things operate the way they do for a reason, regardless of whether it is a good reason. While you may be the answer to all their problems, you are far too new to fully understand and appreciate what that reasoning is at this point. Now is the time to listen and learn. One day soon, after you have a better clue, you can begin to change things up.

8. Make Notes to Self—Literally

Depending on your learning style, you could find it useful to take notes as you learn the ins and outs of your new position. You may be potentially learning a lot of new things, and that is certainly one way to remember them.

Notes made while you are fairly new and naïve could come in useful later when you want to enhance organizational efficiencies through process redesign, or elimination, too. Those scribbles were made with a truly objective and innocent eye, which is often needed to see past the inefficiencies in the first place. #teamnewbie

9. Remember the Names and Job Titles of Everyone You Meet

Your network is going to continue to grow as you begin your new job. You are going to be meeting new colleagues and customers, both internal and external to the organization. Remember their names and job titles for future use.

If, however, you are like many other people who have a difficult time remembering names, don't stress. According to a Forbes.com article authored by Kristi Hedges, a communications expert and leadership coach, you are not alone, and there are some tricks you can use to help yourself improve on the process:[1]

- When you are first introduced to someone, try repeating his or her name once or twice in the course of the ensuing conversation.
- Ask the person to spell out his or her last name, particularly if it is an unusual one.
- Collect a business card from the person, and, shortly after your meeting, make a couple of notes to remind you specifically about that individual.
- Associate the person you met with an image or a verbal clue.
- Connect the person you are meeting with someone you already know. For example, you meet a new coworker named Ed Smith. What a coincidence! Your cousin also happens to be named Ed and his best friend's last name is Smith. Small world.
- Consciously care enough to remember the name in the first place.

10. Take the Lead in Setting Yourself Up for the Business of Work

Depending on the nature of your new job, you might need to have a few tools on hand to help you get things rolling in the first few days. Whatever those things are, whether access to a computer network, a pack of sticky notes and some pens, or even a uniform of another kind, get them in place as soon as possible.

11. Go to Lunch with Your Peers

While you want to be careful about aligning yourself too closely with forces unknown this early in your new job, you do not want to be perceived as a loner, either. Make a genuine effort to become acquainted with your colleagues. Going to lunch with them gives you the perfect opportunity to do so. Practice the 90/10 rule when you do. Ninety percent of the time listen to the conversation at hand and learn all you can about the way things really work in the organization. Speak only 10 percent of the time.

And while you are getting all chummy with your new peeps, respect the lunch hour. Leave for lunch on time and return to the job on time.

12. Clarify Your Job Responsibilities, Job Priorities, and Chain of Command

You got the job. Yay you. Now be sure you fully understand what the job is all about. Right from the beginning of your new venture, forge a good working relationship with your immediate supervisor. Make sure you understand what it is you are supposed to be doing, in what order of priority, and who you are to answer to in the process. Learn how your boss likes things done, and then make her happy.

13. Figure Out How Information Is Shared Internally

In the military there was (theoretically, at least) a clear flow of information. While your new employer may have pointed out the organizational hierarchy to you in the interview or during your orientation, that does not mean that important information flows that way, too. Your mission, new civilian, is to figure out how it flows within your new environment. Once you understand that, you will also understand how to effectively advocate for your own issues when the time comes.

14. Avoid Office Gossip

Gossip is alive and well in the civilian workplace, and you have to be careful about being around it. During the first three months on a new job, you do not know who can be trusted and who cannot. You do not know who has a proverbial axe to grind or who is one step away from being an ex-employee. While you can't unhear things said around you, you can certainly avoid contributing to any potentially destructive dialogue. This suggestion applies for your off-line and online worlds.

15. Practice Good E-mail Etiquette and Return Phone Calls

If someone sends you an e-mail requiring a response, give him one in a timely manner, even if it is just a "I'll have to get back with you on that" note. Return phone calls as well. It is the little things you do well that can make a long-lasting, positive impression with new colleagues.

16. Avoid Glamorizing Your Professional Past

The temptation to make grand comparisons between your life in the new job and your uniformed life of yore will be great, and maybe even useful. Don't make the mistake, however, of always living in the past. You will know you are doing so when you start more than two sentences a day with "When I was in the military . . ." This will be interesting on some level to new ears for the first three times. After that, it will just get monotonous.

17. Ask Lots of Questions and Listen to the Answers

You can learn a great deal by asking questions about the job, the organization, and the rules for contributing to the office coffee fund. Bonus points if you listen to the answers, too.

18. Nurture Your Growing Network

Even though you may have already made a good impression on management, you still want to continue nurturing your growing network throughout the organization. It doesn't take a great deal of effort to build up the new relationships you are forming. Say a nice word to someone. Offer to help a coworker out when it looks like he needs it. Be genuine, and others will notice and appreciate you for it.

19. Carefully Begin to Build Alliances

Ultimately, you want to avoid getting voted off the island. One way to do that is to build effective and long-lasting alliances with others who know the lay of the land well. You may not begin to do this on day one of the job, but you will want to dip your toes in the water soon enough.

20. Find Yourself a Mentor

It never hurts to have friends in high places. Having a mentor who is well established within the organization, particularly as you begin your civilian chapter in life, isn't a bad idea at all. Bonus points if you can find one who has successfully transitioned from military life into private industry and can show you some genuinely applicable tips and tricks.

Aside from feeling like you have a proverbial ace up your sleeves, having a mentor can provide you with many benefits. According to Management Mentors (www.management-mentors.com), having a mentor increases your self-confidence and helps you to take better control of your career. Having a trusted mentor could show you how to have your own voice within the organization and how to accept constructive feedback in your new role and communicate effectively. Of course, it also provides you with an important networking contact, but, more important, it can help you navigate uncharted waters, better understanding written and unwritten rules of your new road.[2]

21. Be Willing to Go Above and Beyond

In the beginning, you will, of course, be focused on learning the ins and outs of your new job. At some point, you are going to start feeling comfortable enough to step up your pace. Be careful about overstepping your boundaries, but show that you are ready, willing, and able to step outside of your job description when the time is right.

22. Stay in Contact with Your New Boss

You don't want to go to him or her with every single thought, question, or concern. You do, however, want to establish a good working relationship. Keep in touch with your new supervisor, particularly as you begin to feel the fit of the job itself. Make sure you and your new rater are simpatico on all big-picture issues.

23. Keep Your Resume Updated

Now that you are gainfully employed, you might assume your resume is not as important to you as when you were looking for a job. You are wrong. It is still important. It is even more important now because its content is changing by the day. Make the effort to keep it current because you never know when you will need it on a moment's notice.

Examples of such situations include:

- You get fired/laid off/downsized/rightsized, and you need a new job pronto.
- You get nominated for an award at work and need to provide bio details.
- You want to apply for a new and improved job with your current employer.
- You want to apply for a new and improved employer.
- You want to promote yourself as an expert in your career field.
- You want to maintain an accurate account of your experiences, qualifications, and achievements for your own career-focused ambitions.

An updated, ready-to-roll resume will help you through those tight-on-time moments. Keep your glowing resume updated by reviewing and editing it on at least a quarterly basis.

24. Start a "Fix It" or "Create It" List

It is wise to tread lightly in the beginning of a new job. Eventually, however, you will want to put your own footprint on the way things are done. You may not know enough now, but you will in short order. Even if it ends up not making sense later, start a list of things you *might* want to address, change, or revolutionize once you really know what you're doing.

Items added to this type of created list now are valuable, even if they end up being tossed aside later. Why? Because, young gun, you have the benefit of naïve objectivity on the job, which could promote real creativity (and perhaps even profitability) down the road for the organization.

25. Don't Take Sides in Any Office Squabbles

In the honeymoon phase of your new job, you are less likely to notice the organizational fault lines. They are there, however, even in the most successful of businesses.

When squabbles erupt (and they will), avoid taking any sides, particularly in your first one hundred days. You are far too new to the landscape. You only know the story in front of you. There may be a potentially sordid backstory that could have deep and damaging roots. Be like Switzerland and relish your safe zone of neutrality (for now).

26. Listen to Your Gut

Indecisive may not be a term that has described you in the past. You may be working in unfamiliar territory now and find yourself not quite as confident in the decision-making arena. If that lightning bolt of indecisiveness strikes you, simply listen to your gut feelings. They served you well in the military, and they can continue to serve you well as a civilian.

27. Communicate Effectively

Mark Twain once said, "The difference between the right word and the almost right word is the difference between lightning and the lightning bug."

Clarity in the workplace is a beautiful thing that minimizes confusion, saves time and money, and fosters happy relationships, whether you are negotiating global strategies for world domination or simply determining whose turn it is to clean the community refrigerator.

The basics are simple:

- Say what you mean using as few words as possible.
- Mean what you say and know what you are talking about.
- Listen to what others say.
- Listen to what others don't say as well.

28. Recognize When You Need New Skills and Get Them

You may be unfamiliar with some of the skills needed to succeed in your new job or to advance to the next level. If you are, learn them. You cannot improve professionally if you don't. The idea here is to grow into a better whatever-you-have-decided-to-be in this so-called real world.

29. Manage Your Time Effectively

Ben Franklin advises us from history even today with the following quote: "Do not squander time. That is the stuff life is made of."

How you manage your time in your new job will either haunt you or uplift you to higher levels of productivity and, ultimately, career success. The choice is yours.

There are many books written on the subject of time management, and you should read them if this is a weak spot of yours. If, however, you find yourself ironically short on time, soak in these SparkNotes-like tips:

- Focus on the tasks that matter the most first. If you aren't sure what those are, ask your supervisor for clarification.
- Ditch unnecessary tasks. If a task doesn't need to be done, then don't do it.
- Learn to say no when others ask you to do them favors and doing those favors would interfere with you finishing your own work.
- Forget the concept of multitasking; it's so nineties, anyway. Instead, genuinely focus on one task at hand. Give it your undivided attention and knock it out, or at least move it to the next level where you can pick it up later.
- Learn to distinguish between information you need to know and noise. There is sometimes a lot of loud noise that you don't need to concern yourself with in order to accomplish a given task.
- Figure out the distractors in your life and get rid of them.
- Avoid becoming overwhelmed by the big picture, if there is one. Focus on eating that elephant one bit at a time.
- Center yourself. Don't forget to breathe purposely. Take care of yourself physically, and you'll take care of yourself professionally, too.

30. Be Prepared for Meetings

Love them or hate them, meetings may be a cruel reality in your new job. They don't have to be a major time suck, however, if you take the time to prepare for them in advance.

How exactly?

- Know what the meeting is about before you show up.
- Have thoughtful and relevant questions ready to ask when you get there.
- Know who is going to be at the meeting and why.
- Be ready to actively participate in the meeting and take notes if necessary.
- Don't contribute to the time-collective, time-wasting chatter that prolongs meetings unnecessarily.

31. Identify Ways You Can Potentially Grow the Company's Bottom Line

Know what drives your employer's success and do your best to add to that. You may be able to accomplish this task by thinking outside the usual box.

For example, if your company is in the business of making money through sales, can you tap into an alternative customer or type of customer that could result in increased profits? Can you find ways to streamline existing processes and save your employer money? Can you identify overhead costs that are unnecessary?

Find ways to save or get more cold hard cash, and you will be the up-and-coming company poster child.

32. Don't Look for Love in All the Wrong Places

You might know a friend of a friend who was able to be in an actual romantic relationship with a coworker and live to tell about it. Those stories are the exception, not the norm. Many employers have strict rules about such matters, and for good reason. When relationships go south, they can sometimes wreak havoc at work, too. Best advice? Keep your love life separate from your work life, and you'll be doing yourself (and everyone around you) a big favor.

33. Avoid Using Work Supplies for Personal Reasons

You may have formed an attachment to your shiny new stack of sticky notes, but keep them on your desk at work where they belong. Employee theft, whether intentional or mindless, costs employers about $40 billion annually,[3] and it's a surefire way to find yourself back in the job market without a good recommendation from your former boss.

34. Watch What You Say about Work When You Are Not at Work, Online or Otherwise

Now more than ever before, personal and professional worlds have a tendency to collide. Remember that before you rant about your coworker or your boss, online or off. If you make unprofessional comments, intentionally or not, it could cost you the job you worked so hard to find.

35. Accept That Civilian Levels of Responsibility May Differ from Those You're Accustomed to in the Military

In uniform, you may have been responsible for many lives and lots of expensive equipment. Out of uniform, that may not be the case at all. If you are in charge of the supply cabinet, that might be a fairly big deal in this brave new world, which could take some getting used to.

36. Work Effectively Across Generations

With five different generations coexisting in the civilian workforce today, it is no wonder that miscommunication, misunderstandings, and mishaps occur. Every generation, if stereotypes are to be believed, has its own ideas about work.

According to one *Wall Street Journal* article, "Baby Boomers, born between 1946 and 1964, are competitive and think workers should pay their dues. . . . Gen Xers, born between 1965 and 1977, are more likely to be skeptical and independent minded. Gen Ys—also known as Millennials—were born in 1978 or later and like teamwork, feedback and technology."[4]

In the military you worked well around the generations. You understood that everyone had his or her own learning style and style of communication. The same holds true for life outside of the military.

37. Start Your New Job with a Good Attitude

A good attitude on the job can make all the difference in the world. You are in the honeymoon phase of the job, so milk that good attitude for all it is worth at this point. You will make a good impression on others in the process.

38. Be a Team Player

Teamwork makes the dream work. You know it, so embrace it.

If you need any more reasons to play well with others, consider that teamwork encourages creative thought and learning on the job. It allows employees to build on the talents of their teammates, and it builds organizational trust. Teamwork also serves to teach employees effective conflict resolution skills. It promotes a wider sense of project or idea ownership and encourages healthy risk taking.[5]

39. Develop a Reputation as Someone Who Can Be Depended Upon

Be honest. This should be a total no-brainer for you. In the military, you were known as someone who could be depended on. Carry that same quality with you as a civilian wonk on the job. Complete your tasks on or ahead of time. Help others out with theirs.

Some things transition more easily than others.

40. Minimize Personal Disruptions on the Job

There will be times you will have to miss work. Your kid will get sick. Your car will break down. The snow will be deep. Life happens, and good employers understand that. They tolerate it, but chances are they won't tolerate quite so well it if happens all the time.

41. Socialize with Your Coworkers

You don't have to go out with your coworkers to each and every happy hour, but it won't hurt to be an occasional joiner. It is often during those off-site, off-the-clock ventures that true alliances and professional friendships are formed. Don't miss out on those valuable opportunities to bond with your peers.

42. Show Appreciation to Others

As a newbie on the job, you are likely to be asking others quite a few questions in the first three months. Show your gratitude and appreciation to those who help you because a heartfelt thank-you will go a long way in the short and long terms. People like to be shown appreciation because it makes them feel valued. When they feel valued, they are more likely to help you out when you need it the most.

43. Organize Your Workspace

A messy desk may be the sign of true genius, but a fairly organized one will create a happier and stress-free work environment for you and the coworkers forced to coexist with you.

A clean and tidy workspace, whether it comes naturally to you or not, shows others that you take pride in your work. It creates a sense of professionalism and prevents the room from becoming an occupational hazard.

44. Own Up to Mistakes You Make

You may be incredible, but you are not infallible. You will eventually make mistakes in your new job. When you do, own up to them. Ask someone how you can correct those errors and learn from the experience.

AFTER THE HONEYMOON IS OVER

The first few months of working on a new job can be like a honeymoon. You are in a new relationship, and it seems like everything is so interesting and enlightening. Over time, the newness fades and the excitement is replaced with routine.

In other words, the honeymoon is over, and it might be time for a reality check.

Reevaluate Your Job

Before you accepted this particular job, you thought long and hard about whether it offered what you wanted—on the surface, anyway. Now that you have been around for a few months, do you feel like you made the right decision?

Here are some other questions to think about as you reevaluate things:

Is the job everything you thought it would be? Why or why not?

Are you working in the job you assumed you were hired for?

What do you like about it? What do you dislike about it?

Are the dislikes big enough to be deal breakers?

Do you get the real sense that you have a future with this employer?

Plan for Your Professional Growth

Hopefully, you are fortunate enough to work for an employer that cares about your continued professional development and offers you real opportunity for growth.

Whether you are or are not, however, commit to being the fair guardian of your own growth. No one cares about your future marketability more than you will when you need to have it. With that in mind, create your own career advancement plan and start working it.

- Assess where you are now and where you want to end up.
- Identify any missing skills, credentials, or certificates that can help you move forward, and figure out how to obtain them.
- Give yourself deadlines for obtaining those missing-in-action resume blurbs and hold yourself accountable to the game plan.
- Chart your career milestones and review your progress routinely. Be willing to adjust that game plan if need be for personal or professional reasons.

Continue Building Networking Relationships

Growing and working your network aren't tasks solely relegated to the job search time frames in your life. Relationship building and growing is something you should continue to do every single day of your professional life. Don't get lazy.

Have Courage and Change Course If Your Gut Tells You To

Winston Churchill said it best: "Success is not final; failure is not fatal: it is the courage to continue that counts."

If you should ever find yourself in a place professionally where you are not happy or the job just doesn't fit with your life or who you have become, then be brave enough to move on (or to at least give the matter serious thought). Change never stops, so don't let it or the fear of it stop you.

You may not have to take a massive leap into a new job. Maybe you have a weird preference for paying your mortgage and other bills on time and you like having a steady income. You could discreetly plan your ultimate departure in stages to make it less painful for you.

The point is, you only live once. While what you do should not be your sole source of identity in life, what you do should bring you some degree of professional satisfaction.

Your work should be meaningful to you. If it's not feeling that way now, figure out why and fix it, even if fixing it means bravely charting a whole new course.

Don't Forget to Continue Planning for Your Retirement

What kind of book would this be if we didn't bring things back around in a full circle?

We have already discussed the importance of managing your finances and your own retirement in the military as you transition out of the military. The importance of that business doesn't change when you become a civilian. It just continues.

Much like your professional development, no one cares more about your post-workplace quality of life and sources of income than you. When you are retired from the hectic rat race of life, it is too late to do anything about it.

You can do something about it now.

Conclusion

Not too long ago, as I was nearing the end of writing this book, my handsome husband and I had a nice dinner out with an old friend of ours whom we had met years ago when we were stationed in Georgia. Dave (not his real name) had just started the process of retiring from the military.

Over good Colorado IPAs and bison done right, the conversation focused for a bit on the many big decisions that Dave had to make in the near future and how those changes could affect him and his family. It was a nice conversation, even though there was clearly so much uncertainty attached to it for our old friend.

Like many soon-to-be civilians in a similar boat, Dave had lots of potential plans and ideas for how he wanted to see the transition year ahead of him play out. He also had a cursory vision for how his ultimate retirement years down the road would look. He seemed to understand that decisions he was making now would determine whether those long-term plans would ever see the light of day.

Dave established a vague timeline in his mind for doing the many things he wanted to do for himself post-uniform, which included exciting bucket-list-like things that he and his family had been putting off for years because of his military commitment. And rest. It included a period of precious, well-deserved time to simply decompress from what had been a high, op-tempo career and life for the last twenty-plus years.

He was a little worried how the timing of enjoying those adventures and desired time off could affect his prospects for landing a good job right out of uniform, while theoretically he was at his most marketable moment. Would potential employers, people whom he knew in the here and now, and who understood what he could offer, forget about him if he followed through with his plan to claim a few months for himself and his family before launching an encore career?

As Dave spoke of the many different possibilities, I was reminded all too well of the anticipation, excitement, and outright fear that comes with making such a big transition.

Having survived a military retirement of our own some years ago, my husband and I eagerly shared our common wisdom with him. By the end of the conversation, I'm not sure if we comforted him or terrified him with our many lessons learned, but he graciously seemed to take it all in nevertheless.

I have to admit, too, after listening to him, that a part of me was relieved that that particular time in our life was visible only in the rearview mirror now. We are proof positive that this, too, shall pass. I suspect that one day in the future, you (and Dave) might even feel the same way.

Seeing our old friend and brainstorming his future with him reminded me (and now I'll remind you) that you don't have go through your transition alone.

When my husband retired, I remember one particular thoughtful friend giving us a long checklist of what to do and what not to do that he had written based on his own experiences. We were more than touched by his kindness, and his basic (yet thorough) list helped us so much at the time—just like I think simply talking with Dave about it helped him, too.

You know, from this book, from TAP, and from others around you, that you have an incredible support system to help you and your family.

In addition to all those resources that reside within the DoD framework of care, you know others who have walked this road before, and I would bet they are willing to share their knowledge with you. Pick the brains of people you know who have been through the military-to-civilian career transition before. *Be a Dave.* Learn from them if they will let you. Your experience will not be exactly like theirs, of course, and you won't have to take any of their well-intentioned advice if it doesn't feel right to you, but that doesn't mean that you can't learn something of value from them that could be applied in your own journey.

When one door closes, another opens; but we often look so long and so regretfully upon the closed door that we do not see the one which has opened for us.

—Alexander Graham Bell

When the time comes for you to leave military life behind, whether you are simply transitioning out after a few years or retiring after twenty-plus years of service, don't spend a lot of time staring at the closed door.

Your experiences in uniform or married to it were hopefully good ones, but they are over now, or soon will be.

It is now time to focus instead on what lies before you.

Of course, this can be an exciting time in your life and in your career as well as a stressful one. The more prepared you are to face the many transition challenges ahead of you, however, the more smoothly things will go for you and for your family during the big change (and afterward).

The intention of *Mission Transition: Managing Your Career and Your Retirement* was to help prepare you for some of the many transition challenges that await you. Specifically, its primary aim has been to introduce you to the new BRS and to encourage you to get past the legacy definition of a *military retirement* and adopt the new long-term concept of *your retirement*, whether it is from the military or not.

I hope this book has helped you to think clearly about your eventual (or imminent) transition out of the military. It is my sincerest hope that it helps you to manage your transition successfully, from checking off the blocks you need to in order to get out to finding a new job, and to not only surviving but also thriving as a new civilian in whatever construct of the world you decide to create post-uniform.

Appendix A
Online Resource Links

FINANCIAL RESOURCES

360 Degrees of Financial Literacy
www.360financialliteracy.org

Americasaves.org
http://americasaves.org

Annualcreditreport.com
www.annualcreditreport.com/index
.action

Bankrate.com
www.bankrate.com

Better Business Bureau Military Line
www.bbb.org/council/programs-
services/bbb-military-line/

BRS Resource Page (DoD)
http://militarypay.defense.gov/blend
edretirement

ChoosetoSave.org
www.choosetosave.org Consumer
fed.org
http://consumerfed.org

Consumerfinance.gov
www.consumerfinance.gov

Consumer Financial Protection
Bureau
www.consumerfinance.gov/service
members/

Defense and Accounting Service
(DFAS)
www.dfas.mil/militarymembers.html

Hands on Banking for Military
www.handsonbanking.org

IdTheftInfo.org
http://idtheftinfo.org/

InCharge Debt Solutions
https://www.incharge.org

Investing Calculator
www.daveramsey.com/article/
investing-calculator/lifeandmoney_
investing/#?entry_form

Investor.gov
www.investor.gov

Investor Protection Trust
www.investorprotection.org

Investors Clearinghouse
www.investoreducation.org

Military Compensation
http://militarypay.defense.gov/
BlendedRetirement

Military Hub
www.militaryhub.com

Military OneSource
www.militaryonesource.mil

MyMoney.gov
www.mymoney.gov

National Financial Educators Council
www.financialeducationscouncil
.org/military

PracticalMoneySkills.com
http://www.practicalmoneyskills
.com

Ready.Save.Grow.
http://www.treasurydirect.gov/ready
savegrow/

Retirement Estimator
www.ssa.gov/retire2/estimator.htm

Saveandinvest.org
www.saveandinvest.org

Savings Calculator
http://apps.finra.org/Calcs/1/
Savings

Smart about Money
www.smartaboutmoney.org

CAREER RESOURCES

American Job Center
https://www.careeronestop.org

Boots to Business
http://boots2business.org

Entrepreneur's Source
http://www.theesource.com/default
.asp

Getting Veterans Back to Business
(U.S. SBA)
https://www.sba.gov/sites/default/files/
files/veternsbackbus.pdf

Hiring Our Heroes
https://www.uschamberfoundation
.org/hiring-our-heroes

Hoovers
http://www.hoovers.com

Institute for Veterans and Military
Families
http://ivmf.syracuse.edu

Military OneSource
www.miltiaryonesource.mil

Military to Federal Jobs Crosswalk
(State of Maryland)
http://www.dllr.state.md.us/mil2
fedjobs/

Newspapers.com
https://www.newspapers.com

Occupational Outlook Handbook
(BLS)
https://www.bls.gov/ooh/

O*Net Code Connector
https://www.onetcodeconnector.org

O*Net My Next Move for Veterans
https://www.mynextmove.org/vets/

Onward to Opportunity
http://onward2opportunity.org/
career-training/

Paycheckcity.com
http://www.paycheckcity.com

U.S. Small Business Administration
(SBA)
https://www.sba.gov

USAJOBS
https://www.usajobs.gov

USO RP/6 (formerly RallyPoint/6)
http://rp6.org/programs/transitionser
vices/

Veterans Career Transition Program
https://ivmf.syracuse.edu/veteran-and
-family-resources/career-training/vctp

Veterans Employment Center
www.ebenefits.va.gov/jobs

Vetnet HQ
http://www.vetnethq.com

Vets.gov Careers and Employment
https://www.vets.gov/employment/

TRANSITION RESOURCES

DoD Transition Assistance Program
https://www.dodtap.mil

eBenefits (VA/DoD)
https://www.ebenefits.va.gov/ebene
fits/homepage

Manpower & Reserve Affairs
http://www.people.mil

My Health (VA)
https://www.myhealth.va.gov

National Resource Directory
https://www.nationalresourcedi-
rectory.gov

U.S. Air Force Transition
Assistance Program
http://www.afpc.af.mil/Transition-
Assistance-Program

U.S. Army Soldier for Life—
Transition Assistance Program
https://www.sfl-tap.army.mil

U.S. Coast Guard Office of
Work-Life Programs, Transition
Assistance Program
https://www.uscg.mil/worklife/
transition_assistance.asp

U.S. Department of Veterans Affairs
https://www.va.gov

U.S. Marine Corps Transition
Readiness Program
http://www.usmc-mccs.org/index.
cfm/services/career/transition-readi
ness/

U.S. Navy Transition Assistance
Program
https://www.cnic.navy.mil/ffr/family
_readiness/fleet_and_family_support
_program/transition_assistance.html

World Chambers Network
http://www.worldchambers.com

Appendix B

Glossary

401(k): An employer-sponsored retirement savings plan.

403(b): A retirement plan that is a tax-sheltered annuity (TSA) for employees of public schools, certain tax-exempt organizations, and certain ministers.

Active component (AC): Service members who are in the regular army, regular navy, regular Marine Corps, regular air force, regular coast guard, Public Health Service (PHS), and National Oceanic and Atmospheric Administration (NOAA) as their full-time occupation.

Active duty (AD): Full-time duty in the active military service of the United States, including active component members and reserve component members who are in an active-duty status.

Annuity: The government's defined benefit or monthly military retired pay that members earn after twenty or more years of service. An annuity is also known as an insurance product within the investment sector.

Attrit: When service members depart or leave military service.

Benefits Delivery at Discharge (BDD): A process that allows service members to submit claims for disability compensation 60–180 days prior to separation, retirement, or release from service.

Blended Retirement System (BRS): This is the modernized and blended retirement system that takes effect on January 1, 2018, replacing the high-3 defined pension system.

Command finance specialist (CFS): The command's principal advisor on policies and matters.

Continuation pay (CP): A one-time payment at the completion of twelve years of service that is available to those who agree to serve an additional four years.

Defined benefit (DB) annuity: A pension plan in which an employer pays a specified monthly benefit upon retirement to an employee based on the individual's earnings history and tenure of service. The high-36 (also known as the high-3) military retirement system is an example of one.

Defined contribution (DC): A retirement plan under which the service member or military service, or both, contribute to an individual account in the federal Thrift Savings Plan that invests in equities and bonds. Benefits are based solely on the amount contributed to the participant's account, plus investment earnings on the money in that account.

Disability compensation: A benefit paid to a veteran because of injuries or diseases that happened while on active duty or that were made worse by active military service.

Disability rating: A percentage assigned to a medical condition.

Disability retired pay: Compensation given to service members who are retired for a physical disability.

Disability retirement: To qualify for disability retirement, the service member must have completed at least twenty years of service creditable under Section 1208, Title 10, United States Code (10 USC 1208), or hold a combined disability rating of 30 percent or more for the disabilities determined to be unfit for military duty. Members retiring earlier than twenty years due to a qualifying disability are not eligible for the lump sum retirement option.

Final pay: A retirement system that bases the amount of pension on a member's last month of pay, or in rare instances, the member's highest month of basic pay. A member must have a date of initial entry of military service (DIEMS) of September 8, 1980, or earlier to qualify.

Financial advisor: A person who gives advice to others about money management and investments.

Grandfathering: A provision in which an old law or regulation continues to apply to some existing individuals even after the enactment of a new law or regulation.

High-36: Also known as high-3. The legacy retirement system that covers members who entered the service on or after September 8, 1980, but before January 1, 2018, who do not elect the Career Status Bonus (CSB). To calculate the defined benefit, the system uses the average of the highest thirty-six months (or three years) of monthly basic pay that the service member received, regardless of whether the time served was consecutive.

Irrevocable: Not capable of being changed.

Lump sum: A one-time payment of money (as opposed to smaller payments over time).

Matching contributions: Contributions made by services to the Thrift Savings Plan accounts of members who contribute their own money to the TSP.

National Defense Authorization Act (NDAA): An act to authorize the government to raise and maintain the Department of Defense.

New accession: An individual who joins a branch of the military for the first time.

Opt-in decision: The choice to switch from the "high-3" system to the Blended Retirement System.

Opt out: To choose not to participate (in this case, in the BRS).

Pay entry base date (PEBD): The date that acknowledges how much of an individual's service is creditable toward longevity for pay purposes. It can be adjusted based on breaks in service. It is referred to by the army as the "pay entry basic date" and by the air force as the "pay date." In federal service, it is known as service computation date (SCD).

Pension: A retirement account that an employer maintains to give you a fixed payout when you retire.

Personal financial counselors (PFC): Accredited counselors who provide information on the Blended Retirement System and offer strategies to support positive financial choices. This service is free to active and reserve components, their families, and their survivors.

Personal financial managers (PFM): Accredited professionals available on military installations to help active and reserve component members and their families understand the Blended Retirement System and support positive financial choices.

Portable retirement benefit: A transferable account when you retire or leave federal service.

Preseparation counseling: The mandatory counseling that service members have to attend in order to transition out of service.

Reentrant: A person who departs federal service and later reenters. Also referred to as a member with prior service.

Reserve component (RC): Service members of the Army National Guard, the army reserve, the navy reserve, the Marine Corps reserve, the Air National Guard, the air force reserve, the coast guard reserve, and the Public Health Service reserve.

Retirement calculator: An online tool allowing users to estimate their retirement benefits under a particular retirement system.

Retirement multiplier: The percentage used in calculating the monthly annuity under the military retirement systems.

Retirement points: The number of points a reserve component member has been credited toward a non-regular retirement.

Retirement service officer (RSO): Army RSOs provide answers for retiring and retired soldiers and surviving spouses. Before you retire, contact your RSO for your preretirement and Survivor Benefit Plan (SBP) briefings. After you retire, they can help with benefits assistance and connect you with retiree councils, Retiree Appreciation Days, and installation retiree newsletters.

Survivor Benefit Plan (SBP): An insurance plan partially subsidized by the government that will pay a surviving spouse and/or child of a military retiree a monthly payment (annuity) to help make up for the loss of retirement income.

Temporary early retirement authority (TERA): Temporary authority associated with force downsizing that authorizes selected members with more than fifteen but less than twenty years of total service for retirement to apply for early retirement. (TERA can also apply to RC, so active service would not apply.)

Thrift Savings Plan (TSP): A defined-contribution retirement plan currently available to members of the U.S. government, including service members. TSP is portable; once vested, the member retains the government's automatic (1 percent) contributions. A member retains his or her own contributions and earnings (and matching contributions, if any) from day one.

Vesting: Grants a member the right to keep automatic (1 percent) contributions (and their earnings) after the member has served two years. A member's own contributions and earnings (and matching contributions, if any) are fully vested from day one. All service counts toward vesting—not just service as a TSP participant.

Working-age annuity: This is defined by the Social Security Administration as sixty-seven years of age. With respect to the Blended Retirement System, it is the age at which the pension returns to a full annuity when the member elects a lump sum option upon retirement (or when he or she first starts to receive monthly retired pay in the case of a non-regular or reserve retirement).

Years of service (YOS): Years of service are calculated based on an individual's pay entry base date; also known as pay date.

Notes

CHAPTER 1

1. Some service members may retire from the military after fifteen years of service for the convenience of the DoD, or they may retire at other times for other reasons (such as medical or command-related ones).

2. Blue Star Families 2016 Military Family Lifestyle Survey, "Benefit Uncertainty" infographic.

3. FINRA Investor Education Foundation Staff, "Understanding the BRS Can Give You a Leg Up," MilitarySaves.org, September 6, 2016, https://militarysaves.org/blog/1400-understanding-the-brs-can-give-you-a-leg-up.

4. "Retirement Planner: Benefits by Year of Birth," Social Security Administration, n.d., https://www.ssa.gov/planners/retire/agereduction.html.

5. Ibid.

6. Extracted from "Policy Highlights," Military Compensation, http://militarypay.defense.gov/BlendedRetirement/, accessed May 4, 2017.

7. "Frequently Asked Questions Regarding the New Blended Retirement System," question #5, Continuation Pay, August 8, 2016, http://militarypay.defense.gov/Portals/107/Documents/Blended%20Retirement/BRS%20Frequently%20Asked%20Questions%208.08.2016.pdf?ver=2016-08-08-092540-300.

8. "Department of Defense: What It Does and Its Impact: How the DoD Shapes the U.S. Economy," TheBalance.com, October 26, 2016.

9. Ibid.

10. David E. Mosher, assistant director for national security, "Pressures on DoD Budget over the Next Decade," presentation at the Professional Services Council 2016 Vision Federal Market Forecast Conference, Congressional Budget Office, November 16, 2016.

11. Deputy Secretary of Defense Letter to Chairman Maldon, November 1, 2013, www.mcrmc-research.us.

12. Karen Parrish, "DoD Ramps Up Training on Blended Retirement System," DoD News, Defense Media Activity, June 1, 2016.

13. Tom Philpott, "Study Finds Good News in Blended Retirements," Military Update, *Colorado Springs Gazette*, February 11, 2017.

14. Military Compensation and Retirement Modernization Commission, *Final Report*, January 2015.

15. Philpott, "Study Finds Good News."

16. Ibid.

17. Marlene Y. Satter, "Military Not Impressed with Retirement Reforms," BenefitsPro.com, January 19, 2016, http://www.benefitspro.com/2016/01/19/military-not-impressed-with-retirement-reforms.

18. "A Survey about Financial Literacy among the U.S. Military," Harris Poll, prepared for the National Foundation for Credit Counseling (NFCC), 2014, accessed May 4, 2017.

19. 2016 Blue Star Families Military Family Lifestyle Survey, "Statistics" infographic.

20. Defense Manpower Data Center, 2013 Quick Compass of Financial Issues Survey, https://www.dmdc.osd.mil/appj/dwp/rest/download?fileName=QCFIA1301...pdf..., accessed May 4, 2017.

21. *Financial Capability in the United States: 2012 Report of Military Findings*, December 2013, page 26, http://www.usfinancialcapability.org/downloads/NFCS_2012_Report_Military_Findings.pdf.

22. "How to Access Financial Counseling through Military OneSource," Military OneSource, http://www.militaryonesource.mil/confidential-help/other-services-and-counseling?content_id=282876, accessed May 4, 2017.

23. https://www.saveandinvest.org/military-everyday-finances/start-spending-plan.

24. http://www.finra.org/investors/what-you-need-know-about-financial-planners.

CHAPTER 2

1. 2016 Blue Star Families Military Family Lifestyle Survey.

2. Ibid.

3. Karen Parrish, "DoD Ramps Up Training on Blended Retirement System," DoD News, Defense Media Activity, June 1, 2016.

4. Ibid.

5. Ibid.

6. Ibid.

7. Defense Finance and Accounting Service (DFAS), https://www.dfas.mil/retiredmilitary/plan/retirement-types/2012-18tera.html, accessed May 4, 2017.

8. Military Compensation, Retired Base Pay, http://militarypay.defense.gov/Pay/Retirement/, accessed May 8, 2017.

9. Military Compensation, Retired Pay Multiplier, http://militarypay.defense.gov/Pay/Retirement/, accessed May 8, 2017.

10. Ibid.

11. DoD BRS Opt-In Training Course, "How the Lump Sum Option Works," page 5 of 8, accessed May 8, 2017.

12. DoD BRS Opt-In Training Course, "Important Lump Sum Information for RC Members," page 5 of 8, accessed May 8, 2017.

13. DoD BRS Opt-In Training Course, "Other Important Considerations about the Lump Sum Option," accessed May 8, 2017.

14. Ibid.

15. DoD BRS Opt-In Training Course, "Defined Contributions," lesson X, page 5 of 5, accessed May 8, 2017.

16. DoD BRS Opt-In Training Course, "Glossary," definition of vesting, accessed May 8, 2017.

17. DoD BRS Opt-In Training Course, "Tax-Exempt Pay," accessed May 8, 2017.

18. "Frequently Asked Questions Regarding the New Blended Retirement System," question #5, Continuation Pay, August 8, 2016, http://militarypay.defense.gov/Portals/107/Documents/Blended%20Retirement/BRS%20Frequently%20Asked%20Questions%208.08.2016.pdf?ver=2016-08-08-092540-300.

19. DoD Opt-In Training Course, "Continuation Pay," lesson 4, page 5 of 8.

20. Ibid.

21. Ibid.

22. Questions and answers adapted from "Frequently Asked Questions Regarding the New Blended Retirement System," August 8, 2016, http://militarypay.defense.gov/Portals/107/Documents/Blended%20Retirement/BRS%20Frequently%20Asked%20Questions%208.08.2016.pdf?ver=2016-08-08-092540-300.

23. Defense Finance and Accounting Service, "January 1, 2017, Military Pay Chart," https://www.dfas.mil/militarymembers/payentitlements/military-pay-charts.html, accessed January 24, 2017.

24. Centers for Disease Control and Prevention, "Life Expectancy," https://www.cdc.gov/nchs/fastats/life-expectancy.htm, accessed January 24, 2017.

CHAPTER 3

1. Adapted from "10 Tips to Manage Stress," WebMD, November 3, 2016, http://www.webmd.com/balance/guide/tips-to-control-stress?print=true.

2. Ron Ashkenas, "Professional Transitions: Navigating the Emotional Side of a Career Transition," *Harvard Business Review*, April 5, 2016.

3. DoD TAP, "About DoD TAP," https://www.dodtap.mil/about_DoDTAP.html, accessed May 9, 2017.

4. DoD TAP, "Core Curriculum, Transition Overview, Resilient Transitions," https://www.dodtap.mil/core_curriculum.html, accessed May 9, 2017.

5. 2016 Blue Star Families Military Family Lifestyle Survey, "Executive Summary."

6. Ibid.

7. Veterans Affairs, "Disability Compensation: Benefit Description," http://www.benefits.va.gov/compensation/, accessed May 9, 2017.

8. Lifeline for Vets, www.nvf.org.

9. "DoD Preseparation Guide, Survivor Benefit Plan (SBP)," page 89, https://www. sfl-tap.army.mil/acap_documents/about_acap/PreSepGuide_AD.pdf.

CHAPTER 4

1. U.S. Department of Labor, "Veterans' Employment and Training Service," front page infographic, March 2017, https://www.dol.gov/vets/.

2. David S. Loughran, "Why Is Veteran Unemployment So High?" *Rand Research Report*, 2014, http://www.rand.org/pubs/research_reports/RR284.html (accessed May 9, 2017).

3. "Fastest Growing Occupations," *Occupational Outlook Handbook*, December 17, 2015, https://www.bls.gov/ooh/fastest-growing.htm.

4. "Social Media's Place in the Job Search," Job Seeker Nation Survey, 2016, page 10.

5. Ibid.

6. Jobvite Recruiter Nation Survey, 2015, accessed May 9, 2017.

CHAPTER 5

1. Kristi Hedges, "The Five Best Tricks to Remember Names," *Forbes*, August 21, 2013, https://www.forbes.com/sites/work-in-progress/2013/08/21/the-best-five -tricks-to-remember-names/#41fb135f501f.

2. "25 Benefits of Mentoring," Management Mentors, http://www.management -mentors.com/resources/benefits-of-mentoring, accessed May 9, 2017.

3. Gail Sessoms, "How to Stop Office Supply Theft," *Houston Chronicle*, n.d., http:// smallbusiness.chron.com/stop-office-supply-theft-41191.html, accessed May 9, 2017.

4. "How to Manage Different Generations," *Wall Street Journal*, http://guides.wsj. com/management/managing-your-people/how-to-manage-different-generations/, accessed May 9, 2017.

5. Dave Mattson, "Benefits of Teamwork in the Workplace," Sandler Training Professional Development, February 19, 2015, https://www.sandler.com/blog/ 6-benefits-of-teamwork-in-the-workplace.

Index

About the Author

Janet I. Farley, EdM, is a longtime respected career transition expert within the greater military community, having assisted countless service members and their spouses transition from the military to civilian jobs or from employment at one duty station to the next.

As a U.S. Marine Corps brat, a "retired" U.S. Army wife, and a career transition expert, she brings a multiperspective understanding to many career transition challenges that military families face at every stage of their lives.

Farley has authored numerous books, including *Military Life 101: Basic Training for New Military Families*, *The Military Spouse's Employment Guide*, *The Military-to-Civilian Career Transition Guide*, and *Quick Military Transition Guide*. She is a coauthor of the award-winning book *Stories Around the Table: Laughter, Wisdom and Strength in Military Life*.

Additionally, she is a freelance writer whose work has appeared nationally in such publications as *Military Officer*, *Making It in the MilLife* (MOAABlogs. org), *Career Connections* (nationalmilitaryspousenetwork.org), *Military Kids' Life*, *Military Families* magazine, the *Reserve and National Guard* magazine, *Military Transition News*, *Military OneSource*, *Military Money*, ClearanceJobs.com, *Stars and Stripes*, CinCHouse.com, CivilianJobNews.com, *Military Spouse* magazine, *Army Wife Network*, the *Wall Street Journal*, *Sierra Vista Herald*, and the *Citizen Newspaper*, among others.

Farley is a noted employment panel expert for the National Military Spouse Network (www.nationalmilitaryspousenetwork.org). She currently resides in Colorado Springs, Colorado. Visit her online at www.janetfarley .com or follow her on Twitter at @mil2civguide.